In Deep but Never Too Deep for God's Amazing Grace

My Life Story

CALVIN C. GORDON

WESTBOW
PRESS®
A DIVISION OF THOMAS NELSON
& ZONDERVAN

This book is a work of non-fiction. Unless otherwise noted, the author and the publisher make no explicit guarantees as to the accuracy of the information contained in this book and in some cases, names of people and places have been altered to protect their privacy.

WestBow Press books may be ordered through booksellers or by contacting:

WestBow Press
A Division of Thomas Nelson & Zondervan
1663 Liberty Drive
Bloomington, IN 47403
www.westbowpress.com
844-714-3454

Because of the dynamic nature of the Internet, any web addresses or links contained in this book may have changed since publication and may no longer be valid. The views expressed in this work are solely those of the author and do not necessarily reflect the views of the publisher, and the publisher hereby disclaims any responsibility for them.

Any people depicted in stock imagery provided by Getty Images are models, and such images are being used for illustrative purposes only. Certain stock imagery © Getty Images.

ISBN: 978-1-6642-5638-5 (sc)
ISBN: 978-1-6642-5640-8 (hc)
ISBN: 978-1-6642-5639-2 (e)

Library of Congress Control Number: 2022901478

Print information available on the last page.

WestBow Press rev. date: 02/09/2022

Chapter 1

I was home in Washington, DC, on leave from East Germany where I was stationed for almost a year. I was a PFC—private first class in the United States Army. I was only nineteen years old and on my way to a place called, Vietnam, Southeast Asia. After my thirty-days leave was up, which went very quickly, it was time for me to report for duty at Fort Lewis Army Base in Seattle Washington.

My brother Walter and my cousin Larry accompanied me to the Washington DC National Airport. I remember sitting in the airport that day with the two of them waiting on my flight, wondering to myself if this would be the last time I would see the two of them again. Both had already served time in Vietnam and knew what I was in for. They asked to see my military orders to see if they could figure out what part of Vietnam or what unit I was going to be attached to. But they couldn't make sense of the codes in my orders. I wondered if I would be stuck in a bad unit that saw a lot of action; after all, I'd been trained with the best in the intelligence field and was qualified to be attached to a special operations unit. That meant I could be doing almost anything, including reconnaissance—a military observation mission of a region to locate the enemy or ascertain strategic features, which could be very dangerous.

Walter and Larry each tried to encourage me in their own way that I would be OK. But it just wasn't working for me. I was in my dress uniform, as it was the custom for all military personnel to travel in dress uniform. I noticed many other soldiers traveling as well. Some looked like they'd just gotten home from Vietnam. Family members and friends were greeting them and welcoming them home from the war. I saw an African American soldier get down on his knees and kiss the ground. He looked so happy to be home. He got up and hugged a young woman who was standing directly in front of him. She was probably his wife or girlfriend. He swooped her up and swung her around in the air, and then they kissed.

I figured he had just come home from Vietnam, as he was wearing his unit patch on his right shoulder. When deployed to a designated combat zone, soldiers wear the patch denoting their company level or higher on their right sleeves to show which units they served in. He was with the 101st Airborne and was highly decorated.

My brother and cousin walked with me to the gate. Before long I was off to Fort Lewis, Seattle, Washington. I loved taking pictures, especially from the airplanes, so I always tried to get a window seat. I remember taking aerial pictures that day of the Pentagon, Washington Monument, and I think the Jefferson Memorial.

When I got to Fort Lewis, I was told by the processing officer that I would have to take jungle and guerrilla warfare training before I departed for Vietnam. Mock villages that included tunnel systems had been constructed to replicate the elements of Vietnam. I went through the special trainings and got fully vaccinated, which took a few weeks.

After all the training, we were ready to depart for Nam. We came from different units, different states, and different backgrounds. But we all had one thing in common; we were on our way to fight for our country.

We would not be traveling as a unit, as we were replacements for troops already stationed there. Some of those troops we would be replacing had, unfortunately, lost their lives and would be coming home in body bags. Some were injured. And some were at the end of their tour of duty, which was for one year. We would probably never see each other again, except for being together on the flight and spending a few hours together when we first got into country.

The United States Amy had trained us to be brave and fearless and not show any emotions. As we boarded the Aircraft, some of the troops looked fearful. I could see them praying to themselves. I could see some were Catholic, as they were making the sign of the cross at the end of their prayers. Others looked excited about going to Vietnam. And some just made jokes among themselves and didn't seem to express any emotions. I heard another group talking about how they wish they'd stayed in school and gone to college.

As for me, I wasn't up for any conversation. All I really wanted to do was get some sleep. I hadn't sleep at all the night before, and I think I was coming down with a fever and having side effects from the vaccinations. I had to take a least five shots to update my vaccination medical record.

Things got quiet, and before long we were up in the air on our way to Vietnam. I said a prayer to God as I was accustomed to doing each night before I went to sleep. After my prayer, I closed my eyes and went off into a deep sleep.

Arriving in Vietnam

It was hot and humid that morning when we landed in Vietnam around 0600 hours, which is 6:00 a.m., on March 20, 1971. The temperature was hovering around a hundred degrees even before daybreak. I could see the sun coming up over the horizon. We exited the plane after an approximately twenty-hour flight from Seattle Washington. The first thing I noticed were Vietnamese men, women, and children walking along the road, some wearing black pajamas and bamboo hats. Some were traveling on bicycles, motorbikes, scooters, and small buses, moving in both directions. There were busy sounds, with the scooters and motorcycles engines humming and the horns and bicycle bells going off constantly. We had to walk in formation from the airstrip to a nearby large compound. Some of the children approached us, asking for money and offering to sell us things as we were walking. I was surprised that the children were speaking a little English, like, "GI number 1"—which meant you were good. But it they said GI number 10 that meant you were bad. Mostly you were number 10 if you refused to give or buy anything from them. We were instructed in our training to be careful, as some of the children would have explosives on them. As they approached, there was a possibility they would throw the device at you at you and run away. Fortunately, that didn't happen to us, but I was on high alert.

There wasn't a sewage irrigation system in Vietnam, and we noticed people relieving themselves near the rice paddies and on the side of the roads. I heard one of the GIs saying out loud, "I'm never going to eat rice again," and we all laughed. My eyes shifted back and forth. I was on super alert, as I had been trained to be. I was taking mental pictures of everything I saw. I was observing everything and trying to process each detail into my memory bank. I noticed the farmers working in the rice paddies. Some who were just bending and pulling up weeds looked like women and children. Some of the men were walking behind very large oxen with plows attached to them plowing the rice paddies.

The ground was flat in the immediate area, but I could see mountains far away, as it was getting brighter by the minute. The heat and humidity were unbearable. I began to sweat immediately as we walked toward the compound with our duffel bags thrown over our shoulders. We had landed in country at a place called Cam Rahn Bay, which was one of the places American troops processed into Southeast Asia (Vietnam). It was a hot zone, which means it got attacked by the VC (Vietcong, Vietnamese Communists Guerrilla Force) on a regular basis.

When we got closer to the compound, I could see the barracks from a distance. Nearer the barracks, I noticed how different they were from the ones in the States and in Germany. They were built with wood and had screen doors and windows, sandbags surrounded each barracks, and there were no latrines (bathrooms). The compound was surrounded with barbwire fences with beer cans attached to the barbwire so at night you could hear the enemy if they were trying to crawl through the wire. There were also many small sandbag bunkers and a few large cement bunkers that looked like they could withstand a direct hit from a rocket. The parameters were protected by American troops. I saw two in each bunker with M60 machine guns, M16 rifles, and grenade launchers.

There was an awful stench in the air that made it difficult to breathe. Helicopters were flying all around, some landing and some taking off, and sand was filling the air. I heard a couple of explosions from afar. The closer we got to the barracks, the better I could see and smell the outhouse, which was off a distance behind the barracks. Then I figured out what that awful smell was. About six soldiers were pulling out from under the wooden outhouse big buckets of body waste and burning it with diesel fuel; they all had their faces covered with green handkerchiefs and did not have on shirts. I said to myself, *How disgusting burning dung.*

We finally made it to the barracks. As soon as we got there, before I could put my duffel bag down, a loud siren went off in the compound, indicating incoming missiles, mortars, and/or ground attack. Everyone was running to the nearest bunkers for safety. I was the only one left in the barracks. As I peeped out of the wooden screen door, I tried to decide which bunker was closest to me. I had two options but only a few seconds to make up my mind. First, I noticed too many troops running toward one of the big bunkers to my left, which was made of concreate. So I decided to go in the other direction toward a smaller bunker that was round and made of tin, with sandbags covering it. It didn't look as safe as the big bunker, and it was a little farther away from me, but my instinct told me not to go to the bunker with the most people in it.

I was a fast runner and a low crawler, which was very important to staying alive in combat. We trained to crawl like snakes, very fast, keeping our bellies and heads close to the ground to keep from getting shot or hit with shrapnel—steel fragments from the bombs.

So, I made a dash for the bunker that was farthest away from me, which was about a hundred yards. As I ran as fast as I could, I heard the whistling of the rocket over my head. Then I felt this great suction from the rocket pulling out all the air in the area, and as it exploded in less than a second, I dove headfirst into that bunker. I felt the earth shaking as I just buried my face into the dirt, still crawling towards the center of the bunker.

I was trembling. When I looked up with sand in my eyes, I was face-to-face with one of the white guys who'd been on the plane with me. I could see his blue eyes stretched wide open with fear. He was calling out for his mother, and before I could say anything to him, another round came in. We buried our faces back into the ground again. That one sounded like it had landed even closer than the first one. It got quiet for about thirty seconds, and then another whistling of a rocket preceded another earthshaking explosion.

The kid was terrified and kept repeating out loud, "We are going to die." He wasn't the only one crying out loud. I could hear others calling out for their mothers and asking God for mercy during the quiet time between the landing of the bombs. We were alone in this bunker and his panicked state only made things worse for the both of us. I thought for a second about some of the war movies I'd watched as kid, and reality kicked in—this was war for real. My bunker buddy, who was terrified as was I, would not stop crying out. I had no choice but to grab him and tell him to calm down and that everything was going to be OK.

He looked at me, and when the next round hit, we held on to each other's arms as we buried our faces into the dirt. My heart was beating so hard I thought it was going to come out of my chest. My knees shook uncontrollably, and fear almost had me paralyzed. But I had to be strong, especially because this kid was about to go into shock if this kept up any longer. This went on for what seemed like forever but, in reality, was only about fifteen to twenty minutes.

Finally, things just got quiet. We didn't hear any more rounds coming in for about fifteen minutes, so we just waited patiently, hoping it was over and there wouldn't be a ground attack. I thought about the fact that we didn't have any weapons yet because we'd just gotten into country. I just prayed that, if there was a ground attack, the parameter guards would be able to hold the enemy back from getting into the compound. Fortunately for us, the siren sounded again with two short alarms, indicating all clear and no ground attack.

I was still shaking and was beginning to feel extremely sick; I believe it was a combination of the side effects from the vaccinations, being dehydrated, and my first combat experience. I couldn't stop sweating and shaking, and I felt very weak, as if I were going to pass out at any second. We got out of the bunker, and I looked at the guy who was in the bunker with me. He looked really shaken up but a little calmer; his face and uniform were full of sand. I could tell he was embarrassed of the way he'd acted, so I just gave him a pat on the back and told him it was going to be OK. Then I made my way back to the barracks, and he went on his way back to his barracks.

As I was walking, I noticed I had sand all over myself as well—in my eyes, my mouth, and my ears. I began to feel angry toward what had just happened. I felt helpless because all I could do was eat dirt and pray to God the incoming rounds didn't land on the bunker, killing the two of us. I'd never felt so vulnerable in my life. We were in deep, and I knew at that moment that only God himself could help me survive an entire year in Vietnam if this was any indication of what I was to experience in the days and months to come.

I made it back to the barracks, and all I wanted to do was lie down on the bunk and sleep. I knew I needed to drink more water and try to eat something, but water wouldn't stay down; it would just come right back up. I didn't have an appetite, so I would just lay on the bunk waiting for the next formation, which we had to make almost every hour.

A sergeant would stand on a wooden platform speaking through a bullhorn calling out names and service numbers, instructing us which unit we were being assigned to and where to report on base for further instructions and the mode of transportation we would be taking to get to our new units, either helicopter or convoy. My name wasn't called on the first day, so I stayed in the barracks overnight and still couldn't sleep. I still felt sick, but at least now the water would stay down. We got hit several times during the night with missiles and small mortar rounds, and we had to follow the same drill each time. During one of the attacks that night, I was so weak I wanted to stay in the barracks and just wait it out, but I mustered up enough energy to make it to the bunker. Some of the attacks were shorter than others, but each time, it took a toll on the mind.

I truly thought life was over for me right there in Cam Rahn Bay at a very young age. I felt weak, and hope was fading. At one of the formations, a large explosion went off in the rear. This time a missile had made it through without being detected, so we didn't get any warning. It happened so fast we didn't have time to react; we were caught totally off guard. I remember standing there with everyone else, all of us listening and hoping our names would be called so we could get out of that hot zone. Then without notice, we heard that suction sound and a great explosion, and all we could do was eat dirt. Then the siren went off, but it was too late. The round had landed in the rear of the formation, killing six and wounding several others. I kept thinking, *How in the world did I get myself into this mess?*

Finally, on the next day my name was called. I was so glad to be getting out of that terrible hot zone, which I learned later was always a bad place to be and got hit on a regular basis, as there was a big ammo dump located in the compound. An ammunition dump is an ammunition supply point (ASP); destroying an ammo dump that would be a big victory for the enemy.

I was instructed to join a convoy that would be traveling south toward a place called Long Binh. It was a long convoy of two-ton trucks, gun trucks and heavy-duty equipment with supplies and ammunition. I traveled in the back of the truck with other troops. Our truck was positioned in the middle of the convoy, which was so long I couldn't see the front or the back of the convoy even as we traveled around bends. I remember stopping several times because of sniper fire or roadside bombs going off. I learned later that the enemy would usually attack the front or the rear of the convoy. I cannot remember how long it took us to get to Long Binh, but it was at least six to eight hours, possibly longer. Again, I wondered if we were safer back at the compound or on the road. This was my first of many convoy trips. I hated convoys; you knew eventually you were going to come under attack. For this one, I was still sick and suffering from dehydration because it was so hot and humid.

We finally arrived at our new unit, CARA 160th, which was on top of a hill. As we walked through the security gate of the compound, some African American soldiers were standing around greeting each other in a way I'd never seen before. They were doing this strange type of handshake that looked cool to me; as each would finish with one person, he would go to another and do the same thing until they'd all greeted one another. They all wore jungle hats, wide-brimmed hats commonly used by military forces in hot tropical climates, that barely covered some of their large afros and black bracelets made of bootlaces on their right wrists, some thicker than others. They all had unique characteristics. Some were dark-skinned others had lighter complexions, some tall and some short, some had southern accents and others northern accents; and they all acted very warm toward each other. Some wore dark shades to and had green towels wrapped around their necks, wiping away the sweat. The handshake was called the DAP, an acronym for "dignity and pride." Its movements translate to, "I'm not above you. You're not above me. We're side by side. We're together." It was a symbol of solidarity and served as a substitute for the black power salute prohibited by the military.

Now dap is a friendly gesture of greeting, agreement, or solidarity between two people that's been popular in Western cultures since the 1970s. Giving dap typically involves handshaking, pound hugging, fist pounding, and/or hooking of thumbs. During the Vietnam War, 90 percent of those imprisoned in the Long Binh Jail during the war were African Americans; it was in the jail that the handshake became popular among the brothers in Vietnam.

Some of us wore black armbands made of bootlaces, representing the black slave shekels our ancestors were forced to wear on the slave ships coming from Africa. This was an era of Black Power in America.

During this time, there was a surge of interracial violence within the United States forces in Vietnam and other places. Black soldiers embraced their culture, as well as the emerging black politics and its external symbols. In fact, the war in Vietnam was America's first racially integrated conflict. Black soldiers had fought in all of America's preceding military engagements but in segregated units.

In the aftermath of Martin Luther King's assassination, in Vietnam, many white soldiers flagrantly applauded his murder. At Cam Ranh Bay, a group of white men wore Ku Klux Klan robes and paraded around the military base. Black soldiers in Vietnam were expected to endure the sight of Confederate flags painted on jeeps, tanks, and helicopters and sometimes encountered menacing graffiti.

We who were African Americans soldiers just arriving at the unit were taught how to dap, but there were some black soldiers who refused to learn or participate and were frowned upon. However, only a few refused to embrace brotherly love and Black Power.

After we got settled in our barracks, we went through our first briefing. CARA 160th was a relatively new unit being put together to take on special operations missions. We had specialist from different units, and everyone had different skills and specialized training. We had combat engineers, experts in explosives, soldiers from the 1st Calvary Infantry, snipers, and the 101st Airborne. We were assigned to teams and to our weapons and flight jackets, which were worn to protect our bodies from shrapnel from bombs or other explosives. We also received a medical briefing and were told to take two salt tablets and one anti-malaria pill daily and to drink plenty of water.

The mosquitos were bad in Vietnam, and they carried malaria. We were given mosquito nets to put over our bunks; without them, you'd be in big trouble. After a couple of days, I was feeling better. I could eat, and the food was staying in my system. I was assigned to Team Two. There were fifteen of us, six African Americans. Bro Doyle from the South Side of Chicago stood about six feet two inches tall; a very light-skinned, handsome guy, he was tough. Bro Rob and Nixon were both from South Carolina. Bro Nixon was transferred from the 1st Calvary and had been in combat already. He always told us to never take anything for granted. Bro Hinton was from a unit up north. He was a big guy and always walked and talked very fast. He would eat with great speed in the mess hall, in and out in less than five minutes. He shared with us a terrible experience he'd had in the dining hall at his old unit. A mortar round had hit the chow hall while they were eating, and casualties were great. Then there was LC. He was from Mexico, a US citizen living in Texas. He was very short and cool and acted like a brother, always hanging around us and showing brotherly love. Because he was so small, he made a good tunnel rat if we needed him.

The tunnel rats were soldiers who performed underground search and destroy missions. The access holes to these tunnels were breathtakingly small, some measuring two feet wide by three feet deep, and would lead to other connections and trapdoors and zigzagged up, sideways, and down.

The rest of our team was white. Two or three of them acted like hippies, and even wore colorful bandanas around their heads. Our team leader was a sergeant who was really laid-back but had plenty of experience in Vietnam.

In two weeks, we had our orders to go on our first mission. A base that had been overrun by the enemy but taken back by our troops, who were having a hard time holding the enemy back and would eventually have to withdraw. Our job was to go in and try to recover all communication equipment from the command center before the base was totally evacuated. After receiving special orders and security clearances, we were on our way.

We took a convoy midway and then a helicopter hop that night.

The helicopter flight was on assignment to support a team of ground troops engaged in a firefight with the enemy. So, we had to go along for the ride as they conducted their mission. Afterwards, they would drop us off at our destination. The door gunners (the soldiers on the helicopter who managed the M60s and did the fighting from the helicopter and who just happened to be African Americans in this case) looked at us as we boarded the helicopter and made hand signals indicating we should take off our flight jackets and sit on them. At first, I didn't understand why, but it wasn't long before I figured it out. It was remarkably interesting; while flying in the helicopter that night, everything looked dark except for all the lights inside the helicopter. Then suddenly, I could see fighting on the ground—tracers from the ammunition from both sides, the enemy and our troops. Tracer rounds, usually loaded as every fifth round in machine-gun belts, provide essential information to soldiers firing at an enemy target by creating a line of sight that allows them to track the trajectory of their bullets and adjust their aim.

This was my first combat action flight on a helicopter. As we were flying along, I looked at the two gunners. They were wearing these very large, black, neutral alloy helmets with fitted slit-like visors and polarized filters, designed to protect their eyes from the bright flashes of light. They tapped on their helmets hard three times with metal objects, which indicated showtime. We were about to engage the enemy in a firefight.

The helicopter made a hard bank to the left, and I could see the gunner shooting at the enemy on the ground; every fifth round was a red tracer. We dove rapidly and then made a fast turn to the right; the other gunner fired his weapon. I could hear the enemy rounds as they fired back at us, hitting the helicopter. Now I knew why we'd been instructed to sit on our flight jackets—bullets would hit the bottom of helicopter and come through, and the flight jackets would give you some protection.

This was my first experience with an actual gunfight from the air. It was utterly amazing. I didn't know there were three helicopters flying the mission. The first was a Boeing CH-47 Chinook heavy-lift helicopter. Its job was to fly low and draw fire from the enemy, and once engaged, it would just turn on a bright light in the area. The second helicopter, which we were flying in, was called a Huey. It would then go down and make more contact with the enemy as the Chinook moved away, still shining its bright lights on the enemy, lighting the area up like a football field at night.

After we made our swoop downwards we could see the door gunners doing their thing on the M60s. This was amazing and exciting. I could see how efficient the gunners were as they engaged the enemy. I could hear the enemy rounds hitting the bottom and sides of the helicopter. I was nervous, but I made sure my fight jacket stayed in place. Everything happened so quickly. Before long, it was over, and we flew back up out of range of enemy fire.

Then to my amazement, out of nowhere came a Bell AH-1 Cobra attack helicopter that just lit up the entire area with firepower, and it was over just that fast. I have so much respect for the door gunners and the entire air support teams in Vietnam.

We finally made it to our destination, and I was glad to get off that helicopter. I saluted the 1st Calvary Air Assault Teams. We'd survived our first firefight and made it to our destination. We had to stay at this small air base overnight. The next morning, we were picked up by a combat escort team. The gun trucks had .50 and .60 caliber machine guns mounted on top. One of the gun trucks had a big picture of the green Hulk on each side. I remember passing an enemy POW camp and the captives were giving us angry looks through the barbwire cages. I was trying to understand everything that was happening, as it was happening so fast. Dead bodies lay along the roadside, and we received sniper fire a couple of times on our way to the base. But we didn't stop. The gun trucks returned fire, and we keep moving until we got there. Fortunately, no one was hit, and we were relieved to have made it to our destination safely.

Chapter 2

Ten years earlier

The year was 1961 in Washington, DC, which was my place of birth. I was only nine years old. My mother, father, sister, brother, and I were close and loved each other dearly. We had some wonderful times together and, unfortunately, some tough times. During the '50s and early '60s, it was hard raising a family of five keeping food on the table, clothes on our backs, and a roof over our heads. Our parents taught us to do the right things, to always do our very best at everything we did, and to always be respectful to everyone and especially our elders.

We didn't really go to church, but my mother would get on her knees with me and my sister every night and pray with us before we went to bed. She taught us this prayer: "Now I lay me down to sleep. I pray to the Lord my soul to keep. And if I should die before I awake, I pray the Lord my soul to take God bless Mommy, Daddy, and our entire generation. Amen." I got on my knees every night and said that prayer before bed. To this day, I still get on my knees to pray, though it's a different prayer. My father always blessed the table before we had dinner. But if he wasn't there, we would say another prayer together: "God is grace. God is good. Let us thank Him for our food. By His hands, we are all feed. Give us this day our daily bread. Amen." I knew my parents believed in God, because we had a picture of the Last Supper on our wall and another prayer: "Bless this house, O' Lord, we pray. Keep it safe both night and day."

My mother at this time was working for the Laundry Factory

Co., and my father drove a sanitation truck for the Suburban Trucking Co., both located in southern Maryland. We moved our place of residence often and had to live with relatives from time to time. Changing schools was not pleasant for me; I had to fight every time we moved to a new neighborhood and started a new school. It was tough in Washington, DC, especially in the poorer sections of town.

We were now living in a town called Deanwood in northeast Washington, DC, and it was a better neighborhood than any other place we'd lived before. There was a big park with a recreation center. We played all types of sports—football, basketball, softball, and I even learned archery. I loved playing football and was rather good as a wide receiver.

My dad was a good man with a big heart, and I always wanted to spend time with him wherever he went. Some Saturdays, he would let me go to work with him. I would lift garbage cans, throwing them in the back of the packer garbage truck, along with the other guys. They always made me feel good, bragging on how strong I was. At the end of the day, everybody would stop at the local liquor store in Kenilworth, northeast Washington, DC, and get beers and liquor and sit in the parking lot just talking and telling stories and laughing.

Sometimes some of the guys would get a dice game going behind the liquor store. Seems like every time without failure, someone would be accused of cheating, and a fight will break out. Afterward, things would just settle down, and they would just make up like nothing had happened. My dad was a good dice shooter, and I took after him when I got older.

At first my dad would only give me a couple of sips of his beer. But eventually, he decided to give me my very own beer, and I felt like one of the guys. Most of the time, though, I could only drink half of the beer before being totally wasted.

The men loved me. When they got drunk, they always wanted to talk to me about everything. Sometimes, they would get so drunk they would start crying. I'm talking about that drunken, tell-the-truth type crying.

They were all good men, just trying to make a living and take care of their families. But for some reason, they would ask me questions and advice. I think I had a gift but didn't realize it at the time. I could see and understand things that were complicated to them but simple to me. I also had a memory like an elephant and was very wise for my age. I grew up fast and had lots of common sense and streets smarts, and I loved being around the older men.

I was a little different from the other kids my age, but I didn't understand why. I was compassionate and loving, and my feelings would get hurt easily. A group of us, maybe seven or eight, would go to the movies on Saturdays. On this day, we went to see *Kings of Kings*. When they crucified Christ, I started weeping, tears rolling down my cheeks. My friends saw me crying and started laughing. I didn't care about them laughing, but I knew I was different because I felt so sad and could not hold back my emotions.

My dad would sometimes get in trouble with my mother for bringing me home intoxicated. My father was also a big gambler, and sometimes he would lose his entire paycheck gambling, which really frustrated my mother, especially when bills needed to be paid. On the flip side of that, he would also win big-time and would always give his winnings to my mother.

Let me back up a little and talk about some years earlier when I'd just started school. We were living on Eastern Avenue in the northeast part of DC. My first school was George Washington Carver Elementary School. I remember the first day of class like it was yesterday. I was five years old, and my mother and I walked to school together holding hands. We went directly to the principal's office, and she filled out some paperwork. Then we were told which class I would be attending. It was quiet as we walked through the hallways to the classroom. We were greeted at the door by this older black woman who looked like she had an attitude. My mother had a short conversation with her. As we stood at the entrance of the classroom door holding hands, the other kids in class were staring directly at me.

Then the teacher, Mrs. Green, said to my mother that I could stay for rest of that day, and I immediately went into panic mode. I was not expecting to stay in school that day. I held my mother's hand harder and did not want to let it go. I looked up at her with a very sad face and said, "I'll come back tomorrow."

But she insisted I stay and let go of my hand as she walked away.

The teacher walked me into the class and introduced me to the other children. It was a long day for me. I didn't know any of the kids and some of them were making jokes about how dark and skinny I was. Children can be very cruel, and I experienced that cruelty firsthand. I survived that first day and was elated when my mother came to get me later.

My mother was pregnant with our little brother at the time. When he was born, I was thrilled to have a little brother. My sister wasn't in school at the time, so she would be at home all day helping our mother with our newborn baby brother. His name was Aaron Gordon Jr., named after my father. I had gotten use to going to school all by myself at this time, and it was only about a ten-minute walk from home to school. I remember rushing home from school every day just to see my little brother lying in his crib. When he saw me, he would light up with this warm smile, and he'd laugh when I played with him. I loved playing with him, and sometimes my mother would let me hold him for a little while.

Unfortunately, he got sick and had to go to the hospital a couple of times during the middle of a very cold and snowy winter. Back then, we had very bad winters and a lot of snow. My little brother had to stay in the hospital for a few days. Then he was released and came back home. I was glad to see him, and he was getting better.

A few days later, I was running home from school to see him like always. As I got closer to the house, I saw a black ambulance driving away, but I didn't make the connection. I ran in—to find the crib was empty. I was confused. He was always there when I got home as if he were waiting for me. But this day was different. The crib was empty. And I could still smell his little baby scent. I thought maybe he was in the living room with my mother and sister, so I rushed to the living room. When I got there, I saw my mother and sister sitting on the couch with sad, empty faces and tears running down their cheeks.

My mother pulled me close to her with tears running down her face, trying to get some words out of her mouth. But nothing would come out. Then finally it came out in a soft whisper. "He's gone. He died in his sleep."

My mother and my sister had gone into his room earlier to feed and bathe him, but he did not respond to them, so they called 9-1-1. He wasn't alive when emergency services got there. He had died from pneumonia in his crib. I remember just crying and feeling utterly empty—a feeling I would get used to in the years to come. This was a very sad day for me, and it took a long time for me to accept what had happened. But I remembered the prayer my mother taught me and believed my baby brother was with God.

Back in school, I was beginning to act out and would get into fights on a regular basis. We had gang wars during recess periods, which was twice a day. All the boys would line up on opposite sides of the playground and charge toward each other, meet in the middle, and fight. We learned how to fistfight, and I became very good with my hands.

The principle was tough on us. We would get into trouble. But that didn't stop us. We had gang wars almost every day. I think I used that time to release some of the hurt and anger that had built up inside me.

The school was named after George Washington Carver, an agricultural scientist and inventor who developed hundreds of products using peanuts (though not peanut butter as is often claimed), sweet potatoes, and soybeans.

George Washington Carver

George Washington Carver was born into slavery about a year before it was outlawed. He left home at a young age to pursue education and would eventually earn a master's degree in agricultural science from Iowa State University. George would end up teaching and conducting research at Tuskegee University for decades. Soon after his death, his childhood home was named a national monument—the first of its kind to honor an African American.

His early life was amazing. Nine years before his birth (estimated between January and June 1864) on a farm near Diamond, Missouri, Moses Carver, a white farm owner, purchased George Carver's mother, Mary, when she was thirteen years old. The elder Carver reportedly was against slavery but needed help with his 240-acre farm.

When George was an infant, he, his mother, and his sister were kidnapped from the Carver farm by one of the bands of slave raiders who roamed Missouri during the Civil War era. They were sold in Kentucky.

Moses Carver hired a neighbor to retrieve them, but the neighbor only succeeded in finding George, who he purchased by trading one of Moses's finest horses. George grew up knowing little about his mother or his father, who had died in an accident before he was born.

Moses Carver and his wife, Susan, raised the young George and his brother James as their own and taught the boys how to read and write.

James gave up his studies and focused on working the fields with Moses. George, however, was a frail and sickly child who could not help with such work; instead, Susan taught him how to cook, mend, embroider, do laundry, and garden, as well as how to concoct simple herbal medicines.

At a young age, George took a keen interest in plants and experimented with natural pesticides, fungicides, and soil conditioners. He became known as the "plant doctor" to local farmers due to his ability to discern how to improve the health of their gardens, fields, and orchards.

At the age of eleven, George left the farm to attend an all-black school in the nearby town of Neosho. Disappointed with the education he received at the Neosho school, George moved to Kansas about two years later, joining numerous other African Americans who were traveling west.

He graduated from Minneapolis High School in Minneapolis, Kansas, in 1880 and applied to Highland College in Kansas. He was initially accepted at the all-white college but was later rejected when the administration learned he was black.

In 1894, George became the first African American to earn a bachelor of science. In 1896, George earned his master of agriculture and immediately received several offers, the most attractive of which came from Booker T. Washington (whose last name George would later add to his own) of Tuskegee Institute (now Tuskegee University) in Alabama. George accepted the offer and would work at Tuskegee Institute for the rest of his life.

My Story

After that horrible situation with my baby brother, my older brother, Walter, who was five years older than me, was playing basketball and got into a fight with some local guys. One of them picked up a brick and busted him in the forehead. He was in the hospital for an exceptionally long time, and when he came home, he looked extremely different. He had stiches in his forehead, and he often complained about having migraine headaches. It took him a long time to recover, and to this day, he still experiences migraines.

If I lost a fight, he would beat me up and try to make me tougher. I was getting good with my hands and could fight pretty well. Sometimes, I would get into fights with guys who were older than me and would lose the fight. But I'd never give up. I would rather give it my best than to have to face my brother. If he found out I didn't give it my best, he would get on me hard, because he loved me, and we had to be tough to survive.

Eventually my brother got better and was almost back to his old self, with the exception of the terrible headaches. I was glad when he started to hang out on the streets again. The older guys wouldn't bother me as much anymore, because my brother had a bad reputation, and most guys didn't want to fight him.

I remember some of the most embarrassing moments in my entire life. We were living in a nice two-story white house on the corner of 49th and Meade. I was a little older then, and we started to experience tough times all over again. Our water got turned off for about a week. On that first day, my dad came home from work, and he was frustrated. He got some pots and buckets together and was headed out of the door for the nearby park to get some water. I asked him to let me go and help carry the water back. So, he did allow me to go with him. He looked at me and said, "Son, I am sorry this has happened to us, and I will never forget you helping me." We had to make several trips, and I was hoping none of my friends would see us. But if they did, I would have just had to live with it. We had to use the water to bathe in and to flush the toilet.

I also remember a few times when my sister and I would be hungry as we waited for my dad to come home with dinner so our mother could cook it for us. A couple of times, he would come home without any dinner, and we had to go to bed on empty stomachs or would drink sugar water to hold us over to the next day. I hated that feeling, and it caused me to develop an inferiority complex.

Our mother always found a way the next morning to get some food for us to eat. I made a promise to myself then—my children would never go to bed hungry, no matter what.

I had to put cardboard in the bottom of my shoes because of the holes in them. I would always walk behind the other kids as we walked to school because anyone who was walking behind you would be able to see the cardboard and would make fun of you.

When things were hard for us, they were hard. But when things were good, they were good. Things were beginning to look up once again, and we moved around the corner into a big, white two-story house. Our new school, Houston Elementary School, was right around the corner. Most of our friends had to walk past our house to get to school, and they thought we were rich because we were living in this beautiful house. I liked the feeling that came along with everyone thinking we had money. But the reality was I still felt inferior.

Well, the good times only lasted for about a year. Then we fell on bad times all over again, as my dad had lost his job. We went from doing very well financially to struggling all over again and were about to be evicted from our home. We had to go and live with our cousins—my father's brother, Uncle Clifford, and his family in northeastern Washington—and enroll in a new school.

I remember going back to our old neighborhood to visit some of my old friends, and they teased me about getting evicted from my home. My best friend at the time made fun of my situation, and I'm sure the other kids saw our furniture sitting out on the curbside because they had to walk right past our house to get to school.

I was embarrassed and angry all at the same time, but I was happy because I didn't have to see my old friends anymore. Life was up and down. Not long after that, my mother decided she could no longer take the pressure, so she called my grandmother, who lived in Jacksonville, Florida, and pleaded with her for some help. My grandmother sent four bus tickets for my mother, sister, brother, and myself. However, my brother decided he wasn't going to leave DC. He stayed with our dad, who at the time was living with Uncle Clifford and his family.

I really wanted my big brother to come with us, but he had his mind made up to stay in Washington and finish school. He had a girlfriend, Liz, who he was in love with, and they ended up getting married.

Chapter 3

I felt I had to be the man now and take care of my mother and little sister. The three of us boarded a Greyhound bus at Union Station Bus Terminal in Washington DC, heading for Jacksonville, Florida. It was a long bus ride, and we stopped in every state, sometimes two or three times in each state.

I was a daydreamer, and my mind was always running from one thing to the next. As we traveled, I began to daydream about some of the good times in Washington, DC, especially walking down Georgia Avenue in northwestern DC near the Wonder Bread factory when I was young maybe five or six years old, smelling the freshly baked bread. I loved that smell. Those were the good old days, when we had plenty of money and lived in a nice big home in uptown DC near Howard University.

I also thought of times when I would ride in the back seat with my father in his new car as he cruised down 14th and U Street and then up Florida Avenue. The streets were lively and busy, people walking everywhere in and out of stores like McBride and black-owned business, the fish markets and fruit stands, and the streetcars moving in the middle of the streets in both directions. The radio in the car was set to the local radio station, and you could see the DJ through the window as we cruised down 14th street, playing songs like "Ain't That a Shame" by Fats Domino or "Having a Party" by Sam Cooke. As we passed the station, I could hear the D.J. saying, "Here comes Aaron again cruising in his red and grey Buick." I loved that he knew my dad's name; the recognition made him sound so important.

My dad was a big gambler and hustler during the early '50s. I witnessed a lot of things because I was always with him. I was only five or six years old, and I would cry if he wouldn't take me with him. He made me promise never to tell anyone what I witnessed, and I kept everything to myself. I called the police Bo Diddley. As we drove around, I would look out the back window, and if I saw the police driving behind us, I would say, "Dad, I see Bo Diddley."

My dad always carried a knife and kept a baseball bat in the trunk of the car. I remember a time we were coming home late at night. My dad and uncle were wasted; they'd been gambling and drinking heavily. We parked the car in front of our apartment on Eastern Ave., but before they could get all the way out of the car, two men jumped out of their car and started beating them badly. I was scared as I watched my dad and uncle trying but unable to get away from their assailants. They called me Scooter at that time. I could hear them shouting out, "Scooter, open the truck." I was so scared I couldn't move out of the back seat of the car to get to the trunk and push the button that would open the trunk. Eventually, my uncle was able to get to the trunk and get the bat. He started whaling on those guys, and they got into their car and took off. It was amazing to me how quickly they had sobered up. I felt a little guilty about having been too scared to get out of the car and get the bat for them.

My mother came out of the house screaming to the top of her lungs. She was livid that I'd been exposed to that type of violence. Now that I think about it, I believe those two guys had lost their money to my dad and uncle in a dice game and realized they had been cheating using loaded dice. They would drill tiny holes in the dice and put lead on one side, increasing the odds of it landing on a particular number. Usually, it would be set to hit seven or eleven. My dad and uncle were good at switching the dice in and out of games.

As I got older, I always had a hustle making money. When it snowed, we would go out and shovel snow for money all day long. In the summer, I'd go out with a few friends, and we'd find empty soda bottles and turn them in for money. Back then, you would get two cents per bottle. I also got a newspaper route and made good money delivering papers early in the morning before school.

Back on the bus

I was feeling sick from being on the bus for so long. I told my mother I was getting seasick (lol). She looked at me with a funny expression on her face and just smiled. Then my little smart sister, Patricia, laughed at me and said, "We are not on a boat, silly."

I kept on thinking about my dad and Walter my brother, wondering how they were doing. My dad had been drunk and passed out on the bed when we'd left DC. I knew we would need some money. And I knew where my dad hid his money if he had any, so I sneaked into the room and went into his little pocket—I think it's called a watch pocket—and took two twenty-dollar bills that were folded up real small. I felt guilty about stealing, but I figured he would understand. I never shared that with anyone until now.

We finally arrived at the bus terminal in Jacksonville, Florida. As we got off the bus, I noticed a funny smell in the air, like rotten eggs. Later, I found out it was from the paper mills and chemical plants. It was a warm evening around 5:00 p.m. There was a light breeze in the air, and beautiful white sand was drifting down the streets. We got into a cab that took us to my grandmother's house on Church and Lee Streets. I had only seen her once before when she came to Washington to visit us. She was a cheerful, funny person, with beautiful white hair and rosy cheeks. She was Native American. When we got to her home, she was happy to see us, and I was happy to see her. The house was big with a large backyard. She had plenty of plants on the front porch.

Grandma loved to cook. She asked me, "What is your favorite food?"

"Fried chicken," I told her.

That Sunday, she cooked golden crispy chicken, collard greens, white rice, corn bread, and brown gravy—my favorite meal to this day. Dinner was delicious, and I realized where my mother had learned how to fry chicken. That became our regular Sunday meal, after church.

Grandma was a Sunday school teacher, so my sister and I went to church every Sunday, all day long. I remember talking to my brother back in Washington, DC, on the phone telling him we had to go to church every Sunday. I think he laughed at me. After about a year, my brother told me my voice had changed and that I had a Southern accent.

Grandma was proud of me because I was a straight A student, and if I got a B, I would be upset. She loved her Coca-Colas and snuff. She would always send me to the corner store to pick them up for her.

I used to stand in the kitchen and watch my grandmother cook dinner. When she was baking a cake, she'd give me the bowl to mix up the icing, and I got to eat what did not go on the cake. One day, I backed up toward one of the cabinets that she would put the cornbread and cakes on after taking them out of the oven. I burned the right side of my back under my right arm, and that scar is still visible today.

One Sunday morning during the 11:00 a.m. service, the pastor of Mt. Sinai Baptist Church, Rev. Robinson was preaching. I felt something I couldn't explain, but it made me want to surrender my life to Christ. And that was exactly what I did. Patricia, my sister did the same, and we were baptized together a few weeks later. My grandmother was happy, and she shouted for joy.

My mother got a job working at a local laundry cleaning service, and we didn't see her that often. She was busy working most of the time, and I think she'd started dating another man by the name of Mr. Riley. My grandmother was strict and had my mother on a curfew, which did not go over well—it wasn't too long before my mother decided it was time for us to move. After living with grandma for over a year, going to church every Sunday, and doing well in school, I really did not want to move.

Chapter 4

Welaka, Florida

My dad had moved back to Florida from Washington, DC, and was living in his hometown of Welaka. I was happy that my mother and father were getting back together and trying to work things out. I knew they loved each other, but life had been so tough before they just couldn't make it any longer. So, my mother, my sister, and I moved to Welaka to live with my dad. It was very country, with dirt roads and one traffic light in the entire town. It seemed as if we were in a totally new world. There were no streetlights, and at night, it was so dark you couldn't see anything. But you could see millions of stars in the sky, and it felt like you could just reach up and touch them. I felt like it was a piece of heaven on earth. I also saw cows, bulls, chickens, pigs, and other wildlife up close for the first time. This was an amazing little town with a very interesting history.

Welaka town's history

The town of Welaka was originally a five hundred-acre tract purchased by James William Bryant in 1852 and known as Mt. Tucker. Prior to the war, there were large orange groves and cotton plantations. In 1860, Welaka's population was slightly over one hundred. At the end of the Civil War, fewer than twenty remained.

The town grew again and was incorporated on April 23, 1887, and Welaka was affirmed as the town's name. The name *Welaka* is said to have been derived from the word local American Indians used for the St. Johns River. By the 1880s, Welaka had become a resort town, marketing itself to visitors seeking medicinal cures from the mineral water of the local springs. The Welaka Mineral Water Company was incorporated in 1907.

The Gullah or Geechee are descendants of African slaves who lived and still live on the coastal islands and in the low country along the coast of the southeastern United States, from the St. John's River in Florida to the Cape Fear River in North Carolina. Their communities dot the four hundred-mile strip, and they are slowly disappearing, casualties of progress and our love affair with coastal living.

Gullah Geechee is a unique Creole language spoken in the coastal areas of North Carolina, South Carolina, Georgia, and Florida. The Gullah Geechee language began as a simplified form of communication among people who spoke many different languages, including European slave traders, slave owners, and diverse African ethnic groups. The vocabulary and grammatical roots come from African and European languages. It's the only distinctly, African Creole language in the United States, and it has influenced traditional Southern vocabulary and speech patterns.

My family history in Welaka

A lot of my family members lived in this small town on my dad's side of the family, on both his mother's and father's sides. He never got to know his mother, my grandmother Essie, because she passed away shortly after his birth. She had sisters, Aunt Mae who was the oldest, and then Aunt Laura, and many great cousins—Cormeal Donaldson; the mother of Earl, Anna, Brenda, Elliot, and Cindy; Gloria Hayes, Janice Strong, Angeline Smallwood and many more cousins.

On my father's dad's side was my grandfather Buster Gordon. My uncle Toby Gordon was the first black deputy sheriff of Welaka.

My aunt Julia Gordon owned the local café and boarding house. My uncle Cornelius Gordon—who was actually my father and his brother,Clifford's, uncle—was a World War II Army veteran.

When I was a little boy Uncle Neal, as we called him, came to live with us in Washington, DC, for a little while, and he was quite fun to be around; he was always very cheerful. He was a Mason and was a very wise man. When he would drink, he would always sing this little song: "A bowlegged rooster and a parrot-toed hen, they all sleep together but hey ain't no kin." He would always ask my sister and me to take off his shoes as he lay in the bed to fall off to sleep. He was born on April 11, 1922, in Welaka, Florida, to Mr. and Mrs. David (Christine Gordon). David Gordon was my great-grandfather. Uncle Neal was also a commercial fisherman. His sister Aunt Colie, whose real name was Jane Robinson, owned a club on Como Lake. He had four brothers, Hermit Gordon, Alfred Gordon, Tyler Gordon, and Mack Gordon.

My nephew Rudy Gordon, who started working out with weights in his backyard when he was very young, now owns and operates, along with his wife, Kayo, Gordon's Extreme Fitness Center in Palatka, Florida. He began doing boot camps on Saturday mornings in Welaka for about two years, using the town's park to conduct his classes. Then he moved to Palatka and used a park called Hank Bryan Park (aka the Village) and did boot camp classes for another year. He got certified as a health and fitness instructor and, in 2012, opened his own health and fitness center.

Cedric Milton, my good friend for many years, became the first black mayor of Welaka. His father, Mr. Ed, became the first black police officer of Welaka many years before Mr. Milton was sworn into office.

Many of my family members still live in Welaka. Among them are my sister, Patricia Mc Coy, and her children; Troy and his wife, Mae, and her daughter, Tywanda Gordon; and Jerome Strong, and JJ Strong Jordan and Rashard Gordon and his wife, Ashanti, and many others.

My story

Unfortunately, things did not work out between my mother and father. But at least they gave it a try. My mother went back to Jacksonville to live with our grandmother. My sister and I stayed with our father but had to be separated, as the house we'd been living in was no longer available. Pat went to live with our cousin Comeal, and I went to live with Aunt Mae and Uncle Russ. My aunt and uncle had hogs and chickens and a little garden in the backyard with peas and other vegetables. My cousin Earl was living with them as well. He was a few years younger than I was, and I became like a big brother to him. Our birthdays were on the same date. He hated to go to school and would cry every morning before being forced by Aunt Mae to get on the school bus. I had to feed the hogs, and sometimes my aunt Mae would ask me to go out in the backyard and catch a chicken and ring his neck and bring it in so she could cook it for dinner.

I really liked my aunt Mae, but I hated feeding the hogs slop and killing the chickens. I also hated going to the outhouse to use the bathroom. Aunt Mae was my dad's mother's oldest sister. Her husband, Uncle Russ, was hard on me most of the time, and I wasn't too fond of him. He smoked big cigars like most of the men in my family, and he always looked very mean. Aunt Mae asked me to do her a big favor one Sunday evening after dinner. She gave me a small brown paper bag with a half pint of liquor in it and told me to go down the road and give it to one of our neighbors, so I did. I ended up making many trips to different people, not really thinking anything about it. I guess you could say was as a bootlegger at a young age.

I had a good friend, Cedric, who lived next door. His adopted mother, Miss Ethel Carter-Smith, was our school bus driver and was pleasant and always had a nice warm smile on her face.

A group of us young men would hang out together every morning playing marbles right in front of Aunt Mae's house before we got on the bus to go to school. The group included Cedric, little Earl, Seal, Charles Milledge, Gene, Larry, Mel Richard, and Milton, along with a few others. Some mornings before school I would get into a fight with my cousin Seal. I don't know why we didn't like each other in the beginning. I guess one of the reasons could have been he was getting all the attention from the family and other guys, and now, I showed up one the scene as the new kid from Washington, DC and naturally got a lot of attention. But eventually we became good friends. Sometimes, he would win the fight, and other times, I would win. Our group became extremely close. We ran together all the time. We'd play in the woods and the swamps and get chased by wild hogs and see all kinds of wildlife, especially snakes. I was afraid of snakes, though I got used to seeing them after a while, but the snakes didn't seem to bother the other guys at all.

It was an incredibly sad day when Mel Richard and Larry drowned in a sinkhole back in the woods. We were warned over and over not to go swimming in that sinkhole, but we did from time to time. Mel and Larry slipped off by themselves that day and ended up drowning. There were some guys working on the potato farm (migrant workers) in Hasting about twenty miles away, but some of them stayed at my Aunt Julia Gordon's rooming house. Some of them rushed to the scene to save them, but it was too late. The entire town was upset over this tragic accident. I was deeply sad and couldn't stop thinking about my lost friends. Throngs of people attended the funeral at the big white church in Pomona Park. It took me a long time to get over their deaths, and I had nightmares for weeks.

Chapter 5

Jacksonville Beach

Approximately two years later, my sister and I went back to live with our mother. It was the end of the school year, and I believe it was in June. Our mother was now living in a place called Jacksonville Beach, Florida, with a nice man by the name of Mr. Riley. He had a son who lived with him, who was nice, and we got along well. I was fascinated with Jacksonville Beach. We lived in walking distance of the beach, which had a long boardwalk with games and rides and a local movie theater.

After we got settled in our new home, my sister and I decided to venture out. We loved going to the movie theater together, so we headed in that direction. When we got to the theater, we saw a sign in the window of the ticket agent booth that said, "Whites Only." We were so naive we didn't pay it any attention and just gave our money to the cashier. He gave us this long, strange look, but he accepted our money and gave us tickets, and we went into the theater and enjoyed the movie.

When we got home, everyone was worried and had been looking for us. We told them that were at the theater. But they didn't believe us. They asked, "Did they just let you go in and see the movie?" And we said yes.

A couple of our new friends asked us if we would go with them and see if they would have any problems getting in themselves. So, we accompanied them the following week and didn't have any problems. They were surprised and gave us praise for being so brave.

Before long, others from our all-black community started going, and eventually the sign was taken down.

My sister and I did the same with the local beach. People were looking for us on another day, and we were at the beach enjoying ourselves without any problems. Eventually, everyone started going to the beach as well. Some of the locals didn't like our presence and were annoyed, but we kept on going anyway.

My mother's new male friend was a nice person, and he cared deeply for my mother. He was well liked, respectable, and a gentleman. We were enrolled in school that fall. It was an all-black school with all-black teachers.

Jacksonville Beach Elementary School No. 144

The name of the school was Jacksonville Beach Elementary School No. 144, and it had begun in the home of a former slave, Rhonda L. Martin, in 1928 when Martin began teaching African American children reading and arithmetic. With growing enrollment, the Duval County School Board built a schoolhouse in 1939.

The endearing plain brick building is a much-loved piece of architecture even today, especially revered at the beaches. Sixty years after the dedication of School No. 144, in 1999, the Duval County School Board offered the building up for sale while a new building that would eventually house Seaside Community Charter School was constructed on site next to the schoolhouse. Former students started the Jacksonville Beach Elementary Preservation Fund, bought the historic building for $1 and—with help from the City of Jacksonville Beach and Duval County—raised the necessary $86,000 to move the building down the street six blocks to a donated square of land. It took twelve hours to move the building from the corner of Tenth and Fourth Avenues to Fourth Street South and Fourth Avenue.

Today, the schoolhouse is home to the Rhonda L. Martin Cultural Heritage Center. Although there is an understated elegance to its brick construction and long windows, the old was nothing fancy—a simple rectangle that once held four classrooms. With links to a woman born into slavery who went on to teach children in her kitchen, it became known by several names—School No. 144, Jacksonville Beach Colored School, and Jacksonville Beach Elementary.

For generations of black residents at the Beaches, it became a distinct mark of pride, a centerpiece and social center for the community—as well as a refuge during Hurricane Dora in 1964. I must add that I was attending this school at that time. I remember everyone, mostly the men, going down to the beachfront and working to fill sandbags in anticipation of Hurricane Dora. Many people found shelter at our school.

In the days before desegregation, kids came from the streets around the school and a black neighborhood known as the Hill, as well from Atlantic Beach and Mayport. My sister and I lived in Jacksonville Beach (the Hill). The school even drew some country kids from the San Pablo area across the Ditch.

Rhonda L. Martin was born a slave in South Carolina. In 1928, with no public schools for black students available at the Beaches, Martin turned her Jacksonville Beach home's kitchen into a school. More and more students came to her house as the population grew, and by 1939 the county put up a four-room brick building as a segregated school.

Earlier Martin had helped found St. Andrew African Methodist Episcopal Church. Services were conducted in her home on Shetter Avenue until a church building went up in 1912.

My story

On the morning of November 22, 1963, I was only twelve years old. As we were accustomed to doing each morning before starting class at School No. 144, we kids stood and placed our right hands over our hearts and recited the pledge of allegiance. On this morning, as soon as we were done, our teacher was called out of the classroom to report to the main office. When she returned, tears were running down her face. She looked at us and said, "Class, our president, John F. Kennedy, has just been assassinated."

The class began to cry also. It was a very sad day in our history because President Kennedy had given African Americans hope that we would not have to continue to be treated as second-class citizens.

Across the nation, more than 70 percent of African Americans voted for Kennedy. We were released from class that morning. And for the next couple of days, I remember being glued to the TV watching the footage of his assassination repeatedly, trying to figure out why someone would want to kill him. My mother and father had often talked about how good a president he was.

The assassination of President John F. Kennedy

While President Kennedy's motorcade made its way through Dallas during a campaign visit—just as the motorcade was turning past the Texas School Book Depository at Dealey Plaza with crowds lining the streets—shots rang out. The driver of the president's Lincoln limousine, with its top off, raced to nearby Parkland Memorial Hospital. But after being shot in the neck and head, Kennedy was pronounced dead at 1:00 p.m. He was forty-six years old. A generation of Americans would forever remember where they were when the heard about this president's assassination, as it would have a profound political and cultural impact on the nation.

By 2:15 p.m., Lee Harvey Oswald, a new employee at the book depository, was arrested for JFK's assassination, as well as for the fatal 1:15 p.m. shooting of Dallas Patrolman J. D. Tippit. Two days later, on Novemberr 24, Oswald would be murdered by local nightclub owner and police informant Jack Ruby at point-blank range and on live TV.

The Hill

There was a famous club on Jacksonville Beach called the 600 Club that attracted people from everywhere. It was located on what we called the Hill, which was only about two blocks with businesses located each side of the road—two pool halls, a barber shop, a laundromat, Pearl's Diner, and some other small shops. The club had live entertainment every weekend, and people would show up to party and have fun. There were always fights breaking out in the club, people getting stabbed, and even a couple of shootings. I was around twelve years old at the time, and me and some of my friends would sneak up on the Hill late at night and walk between the club and the barber shop, where there was a small window we could peep through to see the people inside dancing and having fun and even listen to the live bands. The club had a jukebox as well, and when the band wasn't playing people would put quarters in the jukebox and play songs like "Sitting on the Dock of the Bay" by Otis Redding, "It's a Man's World" by James Brown, and many other oldies from the '50s and '60s.

There were two pool halls next to the club, and back then nine ball was the game for gambling. I hung out at Pee Wee's pool hall and would just sit there and watch everyone play. When it wasn't busy, the owner of the pool hall would let me practice pool on the tables. He usually racked the balls himself, but one day I asked him for a job sweeping the floor after the pool room closed. He gave me the job, and I was excited to be working there. Eventually, he gave me a promotion to racking balls (I was a rack boy). He taught me how to rack balls, and I got good at doing it. There were ten pool tables, and sometimes it would get very busy. Pee Wee trusted me; you had to collect twenty-five cents per game from the customers.

Sometimes gamblers would get close with me and pay me on this side to rack for them. They would want me to give them an edge when I racked the balls. There are two ways of racking the balls—a loose rack and a tight rack. They played with only six balls, which made the game go quickly, perfect for gambling. The one, two, three, four, five, and nine balls were used, and you had to know how to rack fast. If you were cheating for someone, you racked a loose rack with a tiny space between the one ball and the rest of the balls, making it easy to sink the nine ball on the break. And you'd do just the opposite rack for the other person. The key was to be fast and not get caught. I made plenty of money on the side as a rack boy because certain guys would request me to rack for them even though their opponents kept a close eye on me. I could not rack to favor my guy every break, as it would become obvious what I was doing, which would have been big trouble for me.

Next to the pool room was Mrs. Pearl's Kitchen / Dinning Hall. Mrs. Pearl was a nice, cheerful person. She looked like Mahalia Jackson, and she could cook up a storm. She cooked the best friend chicken and pork chops, collard greens, corn bread, and macaroni and cheese in the entire world, along with all kinds of cakes and pies. As I got older and had a regular job, she gave me an open account, and I would pay her at the end of the week. I was eating well, and I loved to eat.

One day, some of us guys were just hanging out in front of the pool hall shooting the breeze and this guy walked up to us. I didn't know who he was at first. But on taking a second look, I saw it was none other than the man himself, Cassius Clay. He was with a couple of other guys and just jumped into our conversation and really took it over with his charisma. He was funning and full of life. He was only there for a few minutes, but it was exciting to just see him.

One of our friends Jody Ballard, who lived on Jacksonville Beach, was just getting into boxing, and we weren't sure if Cassius Clay was interested in him or not. However, Jody ended up becoming a fighter and having an exhibition fight with George Foreman years later.

Jody and I fought plenty of times. Unfortunately for me, he always won. He was a bully, but for some reason I liked him. After our last fight, during which I gave him a good run for his money, he didn't want to fight me anymore. He had two other brothers, Frank and Clark, and they were all tough guys with bad reputations.

Muhammad Ali

Muhammad Ali, born Cassius Marcellus Clay Jr. on January 17, 1942, was an American professional boxer as we all know. He was also an activist, entertainer, and philanthropist. Nicknamed the Greatest, he is widely regarded as one the most significant and celebrated figures of the twentieth century, frequently ranked as the best heavyweight boxer and greatest athlete of the century while also being known for his achievements outside of boxing.

Born and raised in Louisville, Kentucky, he began training as an amateur boxer at age twelve. At eighteen, he won a gold medal in the light heavyweight division at the 1960 Summer Olympics and turned professional later that year. He won the world heavyweight championship from Sonny Liston in a major upset on February 25, 1964, at age twenty-two.

He became a Muslim after 1961. On March 6, 1964, he announced he no longer would be known as Cassius Clay but as Muhammad Ali. In 1966, Ali, refused to be drafted into the military, citing his religious beliefs and ethical opposition to the Vietnam War. He was found guilty of draft evasion, so he faced five years in prison and was stripped of his boxing titles. He stayed out of prison, as he appealed the decision to the Supreme Court, which overturned his conviction in 1971.

That year, I was in deep in Vietnam but was glad to hear the good news made by the Supreme Court.

The Beatles, Otis Redding, Malcolm, Martin, Robert

Pan Am Yankee Clipper flight 101 from London Heathrow landed at New York's Kennedy airport and "Beatlemania" arrived.

It was the first visit to the United States by the Beatles, a British rock and roll quartet. We would listen to their songs on the radio, among them "Love Me Do" and "Hey Jude."

Otis Redding's "Sitting on the Dock of the Bay" was extremely popular also. Otis Redding died in a plane crash near Madison, Wisconsin, on June 10, 1967.

On February 21, 1965, in New York City, Malcolm X, an African American nationalist and religious leader was assassinated by rival black Muslims while addressing his organization of Afro American unity at the Audubon Ballroom in Washington Heights.

On April 4, 1968, Martin Luther King Jr., an African American clergy man and civil rights leader was fatally shot at the Lorraine Motel in Memphis, Tennessee. He was a prominent leader of the civil rights movement and a Noble Peace Prize laureate who was known for his use of nonviolence and civil disobedience.

On June 5, 1968, presidential candidate Robert F Kennedy was mortally wounded shortly after midnight at the Ambassador Hotel in Los Angeles. Early that evening the forty-two-year-old junior senator from New York was declared the winner of the South Dakota and California 1968 Democratic Party presidential primaries during the 1968 United States presidential election. He was pronounced dead at 1:44 a.m. on June 6 about twenty-six hours after he had been shot.

My story

I always found a way to make money. I worked after school at a place a called Sweezy's Pizza Restaurant. I was taught how to make coleslaw and how to fold pizza boxes, and eventually I helped with taking orders. I also worked as a shoeshine boy at a rooming house across from the Jacksonville Beach bus terminal. Mostly sailors stayed there while they were on liberty from their ships that were docked in Mayport, about twenty minutes away. I had a nice shoeshine stand and made good money shining shoes.

During the summer, I would get together with some of the guys, and we would hitchhike down to a place called Ponte Vedra Golf Course, about four miles away. We would caddy and pick up golf balls from the driving range. I was only around thirteen years old, and it was physically demanding to walk nine holes and even harder to do the full eighteen holes. Back then, golfers had the full bags with all the irons and woods. Some of my friends at that time would sneak on the golf course and swim for golf balls in the lakes and sell the golf balls back to the players. I tried it once and got maybe two or three balls. But after seeing the water moccasins, I decided I would make money other ways.

The city built a new civic center on Jacksonville Beach, and I was able to get a job as a janitor and would work there during the summer. That's where I learned how to use the floor buffer machine.

Another good friend, Cecil Donaldson, and I started a lawn service with one lawn mower. We made enough money to buy a second one and did pretty well.

Later I got a job as a pot washer at an upscale restaurant in Atlantic Beach on the water called the Fisherman's Net. It was a large hotel on the water with three restaurants inside. One of our friends, Billy Kennedy, got several of us jobs there. We would leave right after school and catch the bus to work. After getting off the bus, we had to walk about two miles to the restaurant. Most of the busboys where white, and we all worked in the kitchen as pot and dish washers. The chef, along with everyone else in the kitchen, was black. I eventually got a promotion from pot washer to dishwasher and then to busboy. Billy and I were the only black busboys. We would be assigned to work with a certain waitress for that evening. We had to know how to clean and set up the tables quickly and get the food out to the waitresses as soon as the orders were ready for pickup. It would get incredibly busy, and you had to be able to keep up. I became one of the best, and some of the white guys had a resentment towards me.

One evening, Billy got into a fight with one of the busboys and beat him up badly. The kid was so upset that, as he was leaving work that same evening, he said to us, "My dad is in the KKK, and I'm going to tell him what happened here."

Well, that night, we all were anxious; the kid lived right down the street from the restaurant, and we had to pass his house to get to the bus stop. When we got off work that night, it was dark as we headed toward the bus stop down this long, dark road. Our biggest fears came true. We were chased by the KKK. All we could see was white sheets and torches. We all made it to the bus stop safely. I didn't think they were really trying to get us but just wanted to scare us, and they did just that. We were frightened to go to work the next day, but we did. We made Billy apologize to the kid, and we never had any more problems.

My mother was working at a cleaner's and doing domestic work on the weekends. With our busy schedules, school, and then going straight to work after school for me and her working two jobs, we didn't see each other that often.

My stepfather and she began to have some relationship problems during this time, and things weren't great between the two of them. A couple of times she didn't come home in the evening after work, and before long, I hadn't seen her for over a week. I found out later she was staying with my grandmother in Jacksonville.

One day when I'd just arrived at work, I received a phone call from my stepdad. He said, "Son, you have to come home. Your mother has passed."

At first, I thought it was a dream. I was numb and asked myself, *Did I really hear him correctly?* My mind was running rapidly, and I was thinking to myself, *What happened to my mother?* Or maybe it was a big mistake. And if so, *Where is she?*

The owner of the hotel and his wife, the Andersons, liked me a lot. He got one of the busboys by the name of Jim to give me a ride home. I will never forget that long ride that seemed to take forever. Jim drove an orange Volkswagen Beetle, a popular car at that time.

I will never forget how nice he was to me. I can see his face today; he was a little older than most of the busboys and was quiet and handsome with red hair. We didn't talk much during the drive; it was just quiet and long.

When I got to the house, Mr. Riley was there with Pat, my sister who immediately ran up to me and put her arms around me and started crying. I had to be the big brother for my sister, so I held back my tears. Sadly, enough my mother had really passed. We talked to my mother's twin sister, Aunt Daurice on the telephone, and she verified Mom had passed from double pneumonia. We'd had no idea our mother had been sick.

The funeral was held at Mt. Sinai Baptist Church in Jacksonville, Florida, the same church my sister and I had been baptized in a few years earlier. It was a rainy day in February, and it was difficult for me to walk into the church. My brother had come home from Vietnam, along with my cousin Larry from Washington, DC, to attend the funeral.

Everyone was in the church, but I just paced back and forth on the sidewalk, trying to get the courage to go in. Then I looked up, and to my amazement, my best friend was walking toward me. Johnny Maddox had found a way to get to the funeral in Jacksonville, all the way from Mayport Beach, Florida, where he lived. I was so happy to see him. He gave me a big hug and walked with me into the church, and I felt comfort knowing he was there.

I walked slowly toward the casket and could see my mother lying there looking peaceful. A chill went through my entire body as I got closer to her. As I stood over her looking down, I wanted to cry, but the tears would not come out. I just felt empty inside.

My best friend, my mother, the one who had raised me had gone away. I took a deep breath, closed my eyes, turned, and walked away with my head hanging down, grief-stricken. I sat down with my sister, my brother, and other family members, but I don't remember the service at all. I do remember going to the cemetery and then to my Aunt Daurice's home afterwards.

I often think about my good friend Johnny, who came to the funeral to give me support. We were the best of friends. We played in the band together; I was a snare drummer, and he played the bass drum. We also worked together at the Atlantic Beach Hotel. We had so much fun doing everything together. We learned to ride motorcycles together. Back then, you could rent them from the boardwalk. We started on the Kawasaki 250s and eventually graduated to Yamaha 750s.

Johnny went into the United States Navy after school, and I never got to see him again. Years later after I had come home from Vietnam, I was visiting Florida to attend the homegoing service of my Aunt Laura's husband, Uncle Prince. I thought it would be a good idea to go to Mayport where Johnny lived to see if I could locate him. When I arrived that evening, I asked people about him, but no one wanted to talk to me, as I was a stranger to most of them.

Eventually, I was able to contact one of our old friends. We were glad to see each other. But when I looked at her, I could see in her eyes that something was wrong. "You want to know about Johnny, right?" she said.

I said, "Yes. How is he doing?"

Before I could say another word, she started weeping, her hands covering her mouth and tears spilling down her cheeks. I knew then whatever was coming wasn't going to be good. My heartbeat increased as I waited for her to gain her composure. Finally, she looked up at me and said, "Johnny died a few years ago."

She went on to explain that, one evening after he was discharged from the navy, he was walking home, and a drunk driver hit and killed him. It upset the family and community, particularly since the driver of the car was not charged with his death. That bad news upset me deeply. I kept seeing Johnny in my mind walking toward me that rainy day at my mother's funeral.

I gave our friend a big hug. I was glad she'd taken the time to let me know what had happened to Johnny. I spent a little time with her, and we just reminisced. It was getting late, and I had to get back to Jacksonville. It was a long and sad drive for me. Once I was alone, I could let the tears flow. It had only been about seven years since my mother's death, and now my best friend was gone too. I thought a lot about my mother that evening and decided I would go to the cemetery to pay my respects while I was there in Jacksonville.

My mother

Maurice Gordon was born on August 5, 1930, in Jacksonville, Florida, to her parents, Clement and Thomas Smith. My grandmother was a Cherokee Indian born and raised in Jacksonville, Florida. My mother was a twin. Her sister my aunt Daurice was a warm, loving person, and the two of them were very close. She also had an older sister who was my favorite aunt, Earnestine; she always made me feel special. My mother was very intelligent; she'd been a straight A student throughout school and had even learned sign language. She was also ambidextrous.

She was a loving, free-spirited woman and would help you if you were facing any difficulty in your life. She believed in God and would pray to him often. When things were going badly, she would stretch her hands toward heaven and cry out with a loud voice, with tears running down her cheeks, "Lord I stretch my hands to thee; no other help I know." She worked hard to take care of us and to teach us good morals, like being honest, not stealing, being respectful, helping others, and doing no one any harm.

She was very pretty. With a soft medium brown complexion, dark brown eyes, and a youthful look, she stood about five foot seven. She loved to dress nice and wore a unique hairstyle like the women wore in the twenties—the bob, a short, chin-length, wavy cut, often razored and sometimes worn with bangs or brushed to the side. She loved to dance and go to live musical shows at the Howard Theater in uptown northwestern DC. She loved Sam Cooke and Otis Redding. She was full of life, and everyone loved being around her.

When I joined the Boys Scouts, back in Washington, D.C., all the guys had a uniform except for me. I knew we couldn't afford to purchase one, so I didn't mention it to my mother. Then one day she asked me about how things were going in the Boys Scouts. I told her I needed a uniform, and if I didn't have it in two weeks, I would have to stop going. Even though we were struggling financially at the time, my mother found a way to get the money to buy my uniform. She went to her boss and told him about the situation and asked for an advancement on her pay. He was hesitant at first, but she was persistent, and he finally gave in. My mother made me come to her job two weeks later dressed in my uniform to show me off to all her coworkers and to show her appreciation to Mr. Young, who was Chinese and the owner of the company. When I walked into the laundry factory that morning, everyone was looking at me smiling, and my mother had this proud look on her face.

I was fortunate because my mother was able to get me some nice white shirts from the laundry. She made sure I had a nice, clean, starched white shirt to wear to school every day of the week. Some of my friends were jealous and would make fun of me and say things like, "You think you're special."

I was supposed to go home right after school and do my homework and then change into my play clothes before going out to play. However, sometimes I would be in such a rush to get to the recreation center to play football that I would forget to change clothes. My mother would walk past the football field on her way home; if I was out there playing in my school clothes, I would hear her calling out my name, telling me to get home now and change my clothes. I would be playing football in my white shirts, getting green grass stains on them. So, I would stop and run home as fast as I could, change my clothes, and get back to the field to play football—unless she was carrying groceries bags; then I would help her take them home.

I was a little different from my brother and sister. I was a very picky eater. I didn't like watermelon, mashed potatoes, or onions. So, when my mother cooked hamburgers, she made mine separate without the onions. When she bought watermelon for my brother and sister, she would buy peaches for me. My brother and sister didn't like the special treatment I received, especially my brother who would call me a spoiled brat; but he loved me.

I was smart in school like my mother, and she always encouraged me to be better. I always did my best to make her proud of me. I remember bringing my report card home for her to sign. She would just sit there and smile at all the good grades but would say, "How did you get a B? You can get an A the next time."

When she passed away, I felt like my life was empty. I withdrew into my own little private world. I was outgoing and popular before her death, but for some reason that didn't matter much to me anymore. I continued to work and go to school, but it was hard for me without her around. I missed seeing her and would often think about all the wonderful times we had together. When I was around twelve years old, we would walk together holding hands. Sometimes we would just take off in a short sprint race; she would always win. People thought we were brother and sister because my mother had a very youthful look. She would always encourage me to do my best and was very proud of me.

Chapter 6

Integrating Duncan U. Fletcher High School

Things were beginning to get worse between blacks and whites on Jacksonville Beach because there was talk about integrating the schools. A lot of tension was everywhere. I can remember walking down the road and often hearing shouts from white guys driving by in their cars using racial slurs, and sometimes throwing things at us. We had to be careful and always stay alert, especially at night. I remember one evening when the sun was just going down and I was walking down the road on my way to a party wearing my brand-new, red-and-white-checkered shirt when I noticed a car full of guys coming toward me. I could sense trouble, and as they passed me, someone one threw something out of the window and hit me right in the gut. I thought it was a knife because I felt a stinging in my gut. When I looked down at my stomach, I saw it was an egg that had exploded all over my new shirt.

The black students attended Jacksonville Beach Elementary School, which went to the eighth grade. It was an excellent all-black school. The teachers were all black and took a lot of pride in teaching us and showing us how to be respectful, honest, and develop good character. Schools weren't integrated at this time in Jacksonville Beach, and students going into high school was bused to Douglas Anderson High School in Jacksonville.

I was exceptionally good in mathematics, and I joined the band and became the lead snare drummer. After my mother's death, my sister and I went to live with my aunt Daurice and Uncle Shelly and our cousins Shirley Ann and Randy in Jacksonville. I had just purchased my first car at age fifteen years old, a white 1962 Ford Falcon. So, I was able to continue to work at the Atlantic Beach Hotel and stay in school in Jacksonville Beach. I had a friend name Leroy living in Jax Beach, and his mother would let me stay there some days, so I didn't have to commute as often.

Our all-black school integrated with all-white Duncan U. Fletcher High School in Neptune Beach, Florida, about two miles from Jacksonville Beach. With all the racial tension at that time, it was challenging for both blacks and whites. It was clear we weren't wanted at their school, and we didn't want to be there. For the first time, we found ourselves sitting in classrooms with both white and black students together. There were several incidents, fights, and name-calling on both sides.

I had been the lead drummer in my old school, but when I tried out for Duncan U. Fletcher's concert and marching bands, I was told all the snare drummers' positions were filled. The only way I could be in the band was to play the cymbals in the marching band. I knew the game they were playing. They just didn't want any blacks in their band. But to their surprise, I humbled myself and became the best marching band cymbal player. I knew I had to practice patience and humility. Eventually I would work my way up to snare drummer, which was what I was good at.

Our old school, Jacksonville Beach No. 144 made history. We became the first black elementary middle school marching band in the state of Florida—the Marching Seahorses. We went to state competitions and did very well under the leadership of our band director, Mr. Waters, a great person with a passion for music. Mr. Waters was a graduate of Edward Waters College, a private college in Jacksonville, Florida, founded in 1866 to educate former slaves.

Edward Waters College

Edward Waters College is a private, historically black college in Jacksonville, Florida. It was founded in 1866 by members of the African Methodist Episcopal (AME) Church as a school to educate freedmen and their children. It was the first independent institution of higher education and the first historically black college in the State of Florida. It continues to be affiliated with the AME Church and is a member of the Independent Colleges and Universities of Florida. The AME Church was the first independent black denomination in the United States and was founded in 1816 in Philadelphia, Pennsylvania. After the Civil War, it sent numerous missionaries to the South to plant AME churches. The first African Methodist Episcopal pastor in the state, William G. Steward, originally named the college Brown Theological Institute. L Charles H. Pearce was also involved in establishing an educational institution for the AME church in Jacksonville.

Struggling with some financial difficulties, the school closed for much of the 1870s. It reopened in 1883 as East Florida Conference High School and then changed to East Florida Scientific and Divinity High School. Over the next ten years, the curriculum was expanded. In 1892, the school was renamed for Edward Waters, the third bishop of the AME Church. The original Edward Waters College campus was destroyed by the Great Fire of 1901.

By 1904, the college obtained new land, and work was started on the new facility. Edward Waters was accredited as a junior college in 1955 under President William B. Stewart and, five years later, had restored a four-year curriculum. Beginning in 1979, the school was accredited as a four-year institution by the Commission on Colleges of the Southern Association of Colleges and Schools (SACS) and started awarding bachelor's degrees.

My story

Eventually, I transferred to Raines High School in Jacksonville, which was a complete duplicate structure of Fletcher High School in Neptune Beach. I tried hard to keep up with working at the hotel and staying on top of my studies at school, but it just got harder and harder for me to stay focused.

I missed my mother, and my dad had moved to New York to work. So, one day I got this bright idea to stop going to school, leave Florida, and go to New York to live with my dad.

My sister and I were receiving social security checks from our mother, so I asked my aunt to take my checks and use them to take care of my sister and make sure she made it through high school. I really didn't want to leave her, but I needed to get away and, hopefully, find myself before I became completely lost.

I got the details of where my dad was working, in a place called Riverhead, Long Island, New York, from my aunt Laura. I thought about trying to drive my car to New York but decided against that, so I left my car with my uncle and took a Greyhound bus to New York.

Chapter 7

From Florida to New York

When I got to Grand Central Station in New York City, I got on the Long Island Railroad and stayed on the train to the very last stop, but it wasn't even close to Riverhead. I think I was in Brentwood, Long Island, New York. I was out of money at this point, and all I could do was try to call my dad collect. That never worked out though. Every time I called, I didn't get an answer. I tried for a couple of hours unsuccessfully.

It was getting late, and all I could think of was to try to make it back to New York City. It was early evening, and the temperature was dropping. I was wearing a light jacket and jeans more suited for Florida than for New York weather at that time of year.

I was standing on the side of the road at the off ramp of the LIE Highway, 495 West, trying to hitchhike back to New York. I was out there in the cold for hours, and no one would stop for me. I was thinking, *How cold these New Yorkers are.* I couldn't believe not one person would stop. It was getting late, and the sun was going down. I prayed, asking God for help. And before long, help came.

A nice white couple stopped and picked me up. I will never forget them. The wife was pregnant, and her husband was very pleasant. I told them my story, and he offered to give me a ride back to the city. I didn't know it a first, as he was dressed in normal clothes, but it turned out he was a New York City police officer on his way to work.

They gave me a ride to Grand Central Station, and I was grateful for them. I remember thinking to myself as we made our way back to the city that my own people wouldn't even stop to help me, and this white couple had.

As I sat in the back of their car, my hands and feet frozen, the heat in the car warming my body back to normal, I thought, *What in the world was I thinking coming to New York?*

When they dropped me off at Grand Central Station, I had no Idea what I was going to do. I was hungry and tired, with no money and no place to sleep. The only thing I could think of was to try and contact my brother in DC, who was back home from Vietnam. I hadn't talked with him since our mother's funeral. I went to the phone booth and called the operator and told her my sad story, and she tried to locate my brother, without any success.

I was in the Big Apple, New York, stranded at a very young age. So, I went back into Grand Central Station and spent the night on the floor with many other homeless people. I found a little space and claimed it as my own. I had become homeless at sixteen years old. It was a scary situation. A lot of homeless people were hanging around, and stealing and fighting was going on all the time. I couldn't sleep, and to be honest, I was afraid. I had a .25 caliber handgun my friend Leroy had bought for me from a pawnshop in Jacksonville that I kept for protection. I was afraid I was going to have to fight someone or, if need be, use my handgun to protect myself. It was tough times for me. I was tired, hungry, angry, and lonely.

The next day, I went back to the same phone booth and tried again to contact my brother, without any success. The operator told me this time she would do her best to locate my brother and to try back again tomorrow. She gave me her contact information. When I returned the next day, and she still hadn't been able to locate him.

After three nights of sleeping in Grand Central Station, begging for money to buy food, I felt like my life was over at the tender age of sixteen. I didn't want to go to a shelter, as I'd heard horror stories about what happened there, with drugs, abuse, and all kinds of violence. Grand Central Station was all I wanted to even think about dealing with. People were fighting all the time, and I'd witnessed a couple of people getting stabbed. I had to sleep with one eye opened, and I didn't get much sleep at all, except for little catnaps. I was in deep, and I prayed to God for help once again.

I went back to the same phone booth on the fourth day, dialed 0 for the operator, and then asked for my contract person. When she came on the phone after about a five-minute wait, I heard what sounded like sweet music to my ears. He voice gushing with happiness, she told me, "I found your brother." Then she connected me with him. He was working at the main post office in Washington, DC. He sounded happy to hear my voice. I told him my situation, and he sent me some money via Western Union, enough to get a bus ticket to DC and some food.

I was so happy to get in touch with him and to get some food, as I was not doing well begging for money. It was difficult to keep my hygiene up. I would go into the bathroom at Grand Central Station to wash up every day, which was a real task. I was beginning to smell and look like a homeless person.

Finally, I found the local Western Union and got the money my brother had sent to me. The first thing I did was buy some food. Then I went and got my bus ticket for Washington, DC.

Back to my hometown, Washington, DC

My brother picked me up at the bus terminal at Union Station. He and his wife, Liz, were happy to see me. Their son Kevin, who was about five years old, was with them. I was happy to see them and to know there was still hope for me. They lived in southeastern Washington, DC, in an apartment complex called Butler Gardens.

My brother simply said to me, "All I want you to do is finish high school. I shared a room with Kevin my nephew, and he was happy to share his room with me. He and I became very close, and he looked up to me like a big brother.

I enrolled at Anacostia High School, which was walking distance from the Butler Gardens complex. I could see the back of Fredrick Douglas's home from the apartment complex and remembered studying him in one of our many black history classes at Jacksonville Beach School No. 144. I thought it was very cool to be living so close to his home and couldn't wait to take a tour though his house, which had become a historical site.

Fredrick Douglas

Frederick Douglass (born Frederick Augustus Washington Bailey on February 20, 1895) was an American social reformer and an abolitionist, orator, writer, and statesman. After escaping from slavery in Maryland, Douglass became a national leader of the abolitionist movement in Massachusetts and New York, becoming famous for his oratory and incisive antislavery writings. Accordingly, he was described by abolitionists in his time as a living counterexample to slaveholders' arguments that slaves lacked the intellectual capacity to function as independent American citizens. Likewise, Northerners at the time found it hard to believe that such a great orator had once been a slave.

Douglass wrote three autobiographies, notably describing his experiences as a slave in his *Narrative of the Life of Frederick Douglass: An American Slave* (1845), which became a bestseller and was influential in promoting the cause of abolition. So was his second book, *My Bondage and My Freedom* (1855). Following the Civil War, Douglass remained an active campaigner against slavery and wrote his last autobiography, *Life and Times of Frederick Douglass*. First published in 1881 and revised in 1892, three years before his death, the book covers events both during and after the Civil War.

Douglass also actively supported women's suffrage, and held several public offices. Without his approval, Douglass became the first African American nominated for vice president of the United

States as the running mate and vice presidential nominee of Victoria Woodhull, on the Equal Rights Party ticket.

Douglass was a firm believer in the equality of all peoples, be they white, black, female, Native American, or Chinese immigrants. He believed in dialogue and in making alliances across racial and ideological divides, as well as in the liberal values of the US Constitution. When radical abolitionists, under the motto "No Union with Slaveholders," criticized Douglass's willingness to engage in dialogue with slave owners, he replied, "I would unite with anybody to do right and with nobody to do wrong."

My story

It felt strange to me coming back to my place of birth and the place where I'd grown up. Things had changed a lot. The riots had just ended after the assassination of Martin Luther King Jr. Even though I had just missed the riots, I could see the burnt-out stores and all the damage that had been done in our own communities. The same strip where I used to ride up and down with my dad as a little boy was now destroyed, lined with burnt-out commercial buildings. I'd watched on the news when I was in Florida all the riots and the burning down of business in several other cities, like Detroit, Chicago, and Los Angles California, among many more cities.

The riots in Washington, DC

The Washington, DC, riots of 1968 were a four-day period of violent civil unrest and rioting following the assassination of Martin Luther King Jr., on April 4, 1968. They were part of the broader King-assassination riots that affected at least 110 US cities.

On the evening of Thursday, April 4, as word of King's assassination in Memphis, Tennessee, spread, crowds began to gather at the intersection of 14th and U Streets. Stokely Carmichael, the militant civil and political rights activist who had parted with King in 1966 and had been removed as head of the Student Nonviolent Coordinating Committee in 1967, led members of the SNCC to stores in the neighborhood, demanding they close out of respect. Although polite at first, the crowd fell out of control and began breaking windows. Carmichael, who supported the riots, told rioters to "go home and get your guns."

The disturbances began when a window was broken at the People's Drug Store at the intersection of 14th and U Streets, NW. An hour and half later, by 11:00 p.m., window smashing and looting had spread throughout the area. Looting occurred generally where there was little police protection. The local police department could not handle the disturbance. As one officer said, "This situation is out of control. We need help. It's too much for us to handle." The civil disturbance unit was later activated, but by the time order was restored around 3:00 a.m., 200 stores had their windows broken and 150 stores were looted, most of them emptied. Black store owners wrote "Soul Brother" on their storefronts so that rioters would spare their stores.

The District of Columbia Fire and Emergency Medical Services Department reported 1,180 fires between March 30 and April 14, 1968, as arsonists set buildings ablaze.

Back to my story

The corner of 14th and Good Hope Road was the hangout spot, and I had to pass it every day going back and forth to school. You would see people just hanging out on the corner next to the liquor store. My brother warned me not to get involved in any gangs; when I was younger before I left DC, we had all been in gangs.

When I was living in Deanwood at a very young age before going to Florida, we had a gang and fought daily with the guys who lived in Kenilworth, a large, dangerous project complex. There was no school in Kenilworth, so they had to come across the railroad tracks and attend our local school, walking in packs that always outnumbered us. They lived in a tough area known for violence, and they stuck together no matter what. We had some tough guys also, and we held our own most of the time.

We didn't have a local grocery store in Deanwood, so we had to go to the store in Kenilworth. I hated when my mother would send me to the store. If any of the guys from the other side of the tracks saw me, they would jump me. So I had to try and get someone to go with me.

Anacostia High School

I stayed pretty much to myself at school, as I didn't know anyone. And I was OK with that. I would go to school and then come home and do my homework assignments and play with Kevin. There were some girls who lived in the same apartment complex who I would speak to every now and then, and eventually we became friends. Butler Gardens was a nice, little middle-class apartment complex. The young ladies would invite me to go out to parties with them, and I did a few times, but I felt uncomfortable being the only guy with all the young ladies. Eventually, I met some of their boyfriends. I felt like they didn't like the idea of me hanging around the young ladies, so they invited me to hang out with them, which was OK with me. I just didn't want to get involved in any gang activity.

I'd had a Florida's driver's license since I was fifteen years old, so I was able to purchase beer from the local liquor stores. The age requirement to purchase beer in DC was eighteen, but to buy hard liquor, you had to be twenty-one years old. Even though I was only seventeen, once I showed my Florida license, which didn't have my picture on it, the store attendants assumed I was old enough to buy beer. My new friends were happy about that. Now they didn't have to wait outside the liquor store asking older guys to purchase beer.

However, I could only buy beer, so when we wanted harder stuff, we had to get someone to get it for us. We all smoked cigarettes, drank alcohol, and walked the streets, just hanging out, not getting into any trouble.

We started a singing group and would meet on a regular basis to practice songs from the Delfonics, Unifics, Temptations, Smokey Robinson, and many other artists. We got pretty good, and our harmony became outstanding. Our moves were great as well, but we never took it to the next level, even though it was a dream we all had.

I got a job as a janitor at a department store in downtown, northwestern DC. I worked the night shift after school, cleaning offices, emptying trash cans, and cleaning floors. One night after work, I was walking to the bus stop at 9th and Pennsylvania Ave. NW, right in front of the old FBI building. The bus ride took me to SE Anacostia on Martin Luther Jr. Ave, and I would walk home from there. On this night, I noticed I was being followed by the police. I was hoping they wouldn't stop me because I was carrying a handgun. My first thought was that I needed to get rid of it before they stopped me. I could feel in my spirit that I was going to be stopped. I got nervous and tried to move closer to the hedges, but before I could throw the gun away, the officer was out of the paddy wagon and walking toward me.

I had my hand in my pocket with the pistol in my hand and was standing right in front of the FBI building. What a bad situation for me. I immediately took my hand out of my pocket as the officer came closer. He asked me where I was going, and I told him I'd just gotten off work and was headed home. He asked me to put my hands against the paddy wagon and began to search me. Of course, he found the pistol, and I was arrested.

I was taken into custody and fingerprinted. They took my picture and then put me in a holding cell. Later I was questioned by an officer, who asked where I'd gotten the handgun from. I told him I'd had a friend buy it from a pawnshop when I was living in Florida.

Because I was a juvenile, they released me to my brother, pending a court date. My brother had to leave work and come to get me. He was upset and hadn't know I had a handgun. I could see the disappointment on his face when he picked me up. But being the loving brother he is, he forgave me after a couple of weeks.

I was only seventeen at the time of the arrest and was just finishing up my sophomore year at Anacostia High School. I was going back and forth to the DC court, but they kept postponing the trial. I was only seventeen and was still considered a juvenile, but I believe the prosecutor wanted to try me as an adult and up the charges on me. I was happy to find out the handgun was not dirty; after all it had been purchased from a pawnshop. I was going to turn eighteen that July and was still waiting for a trial date, and I was getting nervous I would have to do some time in jail.

Summer was over, and I still hadn't received a court date. I was back in school, but I still had this situation hanging over my head. I felt uneasy about the possibility of going to prison.

One day, I got a bright idea—if I went and joined the army, the courts would have to drop the case. So, I went to the army recruiting office on Good Hope Road, right around the corner from my high school. I shared honestly with the recruiter the exact nature of my problem. He listened intensively and then made a few phone calls. I sat in his office, hoping he'd be able to help me. Eventually, the call he was waiting for came in. As he listened to the person on the other end of the phone, he held my gaze. He hung up, typed a letter, put it in an envelope, and told me to go quickly to the First Precinct. I was to give the envelope to his friend, who would be waiting for me.

So, I immediately got a bus and went to the precinct. His friend was, indeed, waiting for me. After I'd waited in the lobby for about an hour, he returned and gave me the same envelope, now with some additional paperwork in it. He told me to take it back to the recruiter right away.

I rushed back to the recruiter's office and gave him the envelope. He smiled and said, "Today is your luck day." He had my police clearance now, so he could start the paperwork and get me signed up for the military. He then proceeded to ask me questions as he typed out several forms for me to sign.

By the end of the day, I was all set with a date to report to Fort Meade for my physical. This was in September 1969, and I had just started my senior year in high school.

Chapter 8

I shared with one of my good friends, Irving that I was going into the army, and he decided he wanted to do the same. So I took him to meet the same recruiter, and he was able to get signed up right away. We both enlisted in the US Army for three years on the buddy system, which we thought meant we would stay together for our three-year term. However, it didn't work out the way we'd hoped. We only went through basic training at Fort Bragg together.

His mother, Mom Corley, liked me a lot and treated me like one of her own sons. She was loving, well educated, and politically connected in the Washington, DC, area. They had a big family, two boys and six girls. Their father, Mr. Corley, was sick by the time I came along, but he was a tall and handsome man, full of wisdom. He passed while Irving and I were in basic training at Fort Bragg, North Carolina. They let him go home for the funeral, but my request to attend was refused, as he was not my blood relative. I was sad and angry.

I did well in basic training, even though it was eight weeks of pure torture. I survived it and, to my surprise, scored high on all my tests. We were assigned to Alpha Company, with Captain Franks, who looked like Roger Staubach, quarterback of the Dallas Cowboys. He was young and sharp-looking; his uniform was always impeccable. Most of the drill Sergeants were Vietnam veterans, hard-core to the bone. Our drill sergeant name was Drill Sergeant Dallas. He was a little older than the other drill sergeants, but he was fit and wise. He was very dark skinned and looked like a bulldog.

He was from the 101st Airborne and had a lot of combat experience in Vietnam. He took to me and Irving right away.

Most of our platoon members were brothers from DC, Baltimore, Philadelphia, and New York. We all had street mentalities and were tough guys who could talk the talk and walk the walk. Sergeant Dallas was a great drill sergeant. He knew most of us would end up serving in Vietnam, so he trained us hard and taught us how to survive jungle warfare. He went beyond the basic training most recruits received. By the time we were finished with basic training, we had received training equal to or better than the Marine Corps. We scored higher than anyone in our entire battalion on all the requirements, such as hand-to-hand combat, weaponry, mental and physical toughness.

I was young and naive. So when I joined the army, I signed up for the infantry like a fool. I did very well in basic training. I qualified as an expert with the M14 rifle, the M16, and the grenade launcher. I tested high on the Armed Service Vocational Aptitude Battery (ASVAB). After basic training, I was sent to wireman training in Fort Polk, Louisiana, to become a combat radio operator. We trained in the swamps of Louisiana, which they called baby Vietnam because it was hot and humid, and a replica of Vietnam had been set up for training.

We learned basic communications skills and how to call in air strikes in combat situations. As US infantrymen in Vietnam, we had to train with the M16 and or the M60 machine gun and the M79 grenade launcher. And as radio operators (RTOs for radio telephone operators), we had to carry the radios on our backs as well.

I scored high on all my exams and ended up in the top 5 percent of my class and was offered an opportunity to go to advanced communication school at Fort Gordon, Georgia. I accepted the offer, and everyone else except for about five of us got orders to go directly to Vietnam. Radio operators were in high demand in Nam because they didn't last too long in combat.

We said our goodbyes to our comrades who we had trained

with in the swamps of Louisiana and made our way to Fort Gordon, Georgia.

Bus Trip from Louisiana to Georgia

We traveled from Fort Polk, Louisiana to Fort Gordon, Georgia, on a commercial bus with civilians. The bus driver stopped at a station in Arkansas, and some of us went to get off the bus with everyone else to get some water or snacks. The driver told us we shouldn't get off, as, "They don't like colored people in this town."

Some of the brothers, myself included, could not believe what we'd heard and weren't about to stand for it. So we got off the bus and went into the station and dared anyone to say a word to us. There were some guys hanging outside who looked like they wanted to start some mess with us, but they were smart not to try anything. We went in and got some snacks and sodas and got back on the bus and just looked at each other in disbelief that this kind of hatred was really happening. Even our white brothers were upset and probably would have fought with us if we had to fight.

This brings me to a very sad story—about what a World War II veteran encountered on his way home from the war in 1946.

Isaac Woodard

Isaac Woodard was a black World War II veteran who became known to the world as the victim of a horrific act of racist violence that robbed him of his sight. On February 12, 1946, he was beaten and blinded on his way home from the war, hours after his honorable discharge. While that blinding came to define him in the eyes of the public, his life is less well known.

Isaac was one of nine children, born in 1919 to Sarah and Isaac Woodard, Sr., on a farm in South Carolina. Like many Southern African Americans of the time, they were poor and lived as sharecroppers, working land that belonged to whites. As a child, Isaac himself worked in the fields, causing him to miss school. He ended his formal education at eleven years old, after finishing the fifth grade, and then left home altogether at age fifteen. He knew the limits of educational and vocational opportunity for black residents of his native Fairfield County and realized he would need to venture out to find better.

He took on manual labor, laying railroad tracks, log turning for a lumber yard, construction, and delivery jobs. Then in 1939, at age twenty, Woodard joined the Civilian Conservation Corps. He served for two years in the New Deal public work relief program, which provided employment to rural young men during the Great Depression.

In 1942, Woodard was drafted into the US Army for World War II. He was among the more than 675,000 Southern blacks who served abroad during the war, many hopefuls that putting their lives at risk would provide them with a better life and full participation in American society. Isaac completed his basic training in Bainbridge, Georgia, with further training in Pennsylvania, Virginia, and California, before shipping out to the South Pacific in October 1944. He left behind a wife, Rosa Scruggs Woodard, who remained in Fairfield County.

Woodard served as a longshoreman in the 429th Port Battalion, a segregated combat support unit in the Pacific Theater. Loading and unloading military ships in the Pacific Ocean, he helped sustain Allied troops in their fight to recapture New Guinea Island from the Japanese. By the time Woodard arrived in the Pacific Theater, the New Guinea naval campaign had been underway for two years, and Australian, American, and Japanese troops had all endured substantial casualties. Woodard himself came under extensive enemy fire. Though he was not large in stature—at the time of his discharge he weighed 148 pounds and stood five foot eight— Woodard performed courageously and with distinction. He first earned a promotion equivalent to corporal rank and later sergeant rank for his leadership and capability. Ultimately, Woodard was awarded a battle star for service in a combat zone, the American Campaign Medal, the Asiatic-Pacific Campaign Medal, and the World War II Victory Medal.

After being discharged, Isaac was on a Greyhound bus from Augusta, Georgia, to South Carolina, where he was to reunite with his wife. When he asked the white bus driver if he could disembark to use the restroom, the driver cursed at him and refused to stop. "Talk to me like I am talking to you," Woodard insisted. "I am a man just like you."

At the next stop, in the small South Carolina town of Batesburg, the driver called on the local police chief, Lynwood Shull, to remove Woodard from the bus. Shull proceeded to arrest Woodard, beat him with a blackjack, and hit him in his eyes with it. Left unconscious and completely blinded in the Batesburg jail overnight, Woodard was led the next morning—still in uniform—to the city court, where he was fined for drunk and disorderly conduct.

Woodard was eventually transferred to a VA hospital in Columbia, South Carolina, where doctors determined there was no course of treatment to restore his vision. After two months' convalescence, Woodard was escorted to New York City by two of his sisters. The family had moved to the Bronx while Isaac was serving abroad, themselves in search of greater opportunities. Woodard had to begin a sightless life in a new city, with no training for living with a disability.

The NAACP took up his case, however, and Woodard became a cause célèbre when the association's executive secretary convinced legendary actor and director Orson Welles to publicize Woodard's story on his radio program. Woodard participated in events across the country and spoke to audiences eager to hear the tragic story of a military veteran wronged in such an unthinkable fashion. A benefit concert was held for him at Lewisohn Stadium in Harlem, chaired by boxer Joe Louis and featuring speeches and performances by celebrities including Nat King Cole, Pearl Bailey, Canada Lee,

Count Basie, and Billie Holiday. Woodard received a five-minute ovation from the crowd of over twenty thousand when he took the stage to describe his ordeal in a low, quiet voice.

But applause eventually faded, and the public moved on from his story. After two trials, both criminal and civil, that failed either to bring his perpetrator to justice or award him damages, press coverage quickly waned. And once the spotlight passed him over, Woodard was left to fend for himself in obscurity. His wife, unprepared for the drastic detour to their lives, decided to leave their marriage.

Civilian life was filled with struggle and mundanity. Woodard had to fight the Veterans Administration to get benefits, because the blinding happened after his discharge, the VA originally just provided partial payments. Only after writing a letter in 1952 explaining his need for assistance to his VA counselor was Woodard's pension increased to the contemporary equivalent of $14,000 per year.

Ten years after the attack in South Carolina, Woodard's days assumed a quiet rhythm. A 1956 *Jet Magazine* profile on him— entitled "Isaac Woodard: America's Forgotten Man"—described him doing "his morning rounds," waving to neighbors and stopping at a newsstand and local shops. "I make out all right," he said, "but I just can't see."

In the 1960s, Congress passed legislation that gave full disability to service members injured between the time of their discharge and their arrival at home. Woodard's pension increased to today's equivalent of around $45,000 per year.

In 1978, with the help of a VA loan, Woodard increased his real estate investments by purchasing another home in the Bronx. He lived there with his sons, Isaac Woodard III, who he had with a new partner, and George, who he adopted. In the late 1980s, Woodard began having health problems. He died in September 1992 at age seventy-three and was buried with other US veterans at Calverton National Cemetery, in Calverton, New York.

Chapter 9

Uncle Sam gave me an opportunity to go to advance training at Fort Gordon, Georgia. I would become a communication specialist (intelligence agent). I didn't know that this type of trained specialist was in high demand in Vietnam. There were only a handful of black soldiers who were in training with me. After all my training, I thought I was going directly to Vietnam. Instead, they sent me to Germany, where I trained more in the intelligence field.

My buddy Irving was sent straight to Vietnam after his training. He was assigned to the 101st Airborne, and they were stationed up north close to the DMZ (demilitarized zone dividing line between North and South Vietnam). I could tell by his letters he was in deep. He became a door gunner and then a crew chief. I prayed for him every day.

I was stationed at a base called Coleman Barracks in Heidelberg in southwest Germany. The military stockade (prison) was in the same compound. When I first arrived in Germany, we were all living in transition barracks waiting to be assigned to our units. We were at liberty to go into the local city of Mannheim, where there was plenty to do—shopping, good food, and the nightlife. Oktoberfest, which was held annually for sixteen days in September, was full for fun, drinking, dancing, and great food.

My first night hanging out with my buddies at a club called the Pop Club someone slipped some LSD in my drink that I'd left on the table when I was dancing. I went on a terrible psychedelic trip that lasted for over two weeks. This was during the psychedelic era, which LSD and other psychedelic drugs were being used regularly. I was on the dance floor, and the psychedelic strobe lights were on. Things around me started to move slowly and then rapidly. I thought it was just the effect of the lights, but after the lights went off, I was still experiencing the same affect. I felt like I was walking in slow motion. Then I would speed up, only to soon be moving slowly again.

I was trying to figure out what was happening. I grew paranoid as my condition worsened and I began to hallucinate. I didn't want anyone to know what was going on, so I tried to act as normal as possible. I was going in and out of the trips and felt like I was going to lose my mind. Three of my good friends and I took a taxi back to the barracks. I tried to pray to God for help, but I couldn't concentrate on praying. Back at the barracks I went into the latrine to wash my face, and when I looked in the mirror, all I could see was one big eye. This went on for hours. Eventually, I felt like I was coming down from the trip, because the hallucinations didn't last as long anymore.

I felt hopeful that I would survive this terrific ordeal. I couldn't eat or drink anything for days, as I'd start to trip all over again if I smelled food or tried to drink water. It was hard to make formation, but I forced myself to; I did not want to get court-martialed. I was in deep.

Eventually I came all the way down and stopped having the flashbacks. The incident challenged me mentally; I had to fight with all my might to survive. I promised God in my prayers that, if He would just help me, I would stop drinking and smoking cigarettes forever. Eventually, I was able to get settled in with my unit and was doing well with my promise to God. I knew only God had helped me, and there was a lesson He wanted me to learn.

I'd been at the base about three months when a big riot broke out between the black and white soldiers stationed at Coleman Barracks. Angela Davis had come to Germany to speak, but the authorities wouldn't let her leave the airport.

I was leaving my barracks one evening to go to the chow hall for dinner, and all I could see were fights between black and white solders breaking out everywhere. The MPs (military police) were breaking up the fights, and we were all put on curfew. I knew of Angela Davis and believed she was in support of Black Power. What I later learned about her truly educated me.

Angela Davis

Angela Yvonne Davis, born January 26, 1944, is an American political activist, philosopher, academic, and author and a professor at the University of California, Santa Cruz. Ideologically a Marxist, Davis was a longtime member of the Communist Party USA (CPUSA) and is a founding member of the Committees of Correspondence for Democracy and Socialism (CCDS). She is the author of over ten books on class, feminism, race, and the US prison system.

Born to an African American family in Birmingham, Alabama, Davis studied French at Brandeis University and philosophy at the University of Frankfurt in West Germany. She studied under the philosopher Herbert Marcuse, a prominent figure in the Frankfurt School, and became increasingly engaged in far-left politics. Returning to the United States, she studied at the University of California, San Diego, before moving to East Germany, where she completed a doctorate at the Humboldt University of Berlin. After returning to the United States, she joined the Communist Party and became involved in numerous causes, including the second-wave feminist movement and the campaign against the Vietnam War.

In 1969, she was hired as an acting assistant professor of philosophy at the University of California, Los Angeles. In 1970, guns belonging to Davis were used in an armed takeover of a courtroom in Marin County, California, in which four people were killed. Prosecuted for three capital felonies, including conspiracy to murder, she was held in jail for over a year before being acquitted of all charges in 1972.

In 2020, she was listed as the 1971 Woman of the Year in *Time* magazine's "100 Women of the Year" edition, which covered the 100 years that began with women's suffrage in 1920. Davis was also included in the *Times*'s 100 Most Influential People of 2020.

My story

I was trying my best to keep my promise to God, and I did well for a while. Then one day, I decided to hang out with the fellows again. Before long. I was drinking beer and wine and, of course, picked up smoking cigarettes again.

I became friends with this guy from Ohio. We called him Porkchop because he was short and chubby. He had plenty of connections and knew his way around Germany. He had a car and a few friends who were black German women and full of soul and loved to dance and have fun.

Black Germans

In the immediate aftermath of World War II, thousands of children were born to white German women and black American soldiers who were stationed in Allied-occupied Germany. The mixed-race infants were viewed with contempt by many Germans and subjected to constant abuse.

My story

Porkchop and I got close. He was a really fun guy to hang out with, and he loved to drive Germany's Autobahn, the federally controlled access highway system with over eight thousand miles and no enforced speed limits. It was an awesome experience just to be a passenger. But one day, he asked me if I wanted to drive on the Autobahn. I was excited, and my first experience driving on the Autobahn was totally amazing. I drove as fast as I wanted to without worry about getting a ticket. I felt like I was driving on a racetrack, and as fast as I was driving, other drivers were passing me as if I was sitting still. My only problem was trying to exit the highway. There were many lanes, and you couldn't bring down your speed until you were right on the off-ramp. I truly enjoyed that experience and had the opportunity to do it a couple of times again.

We were assigned to the 8th Infantry Division, and mostly we had to spend time up in the mountains doing field exercises with the Tank Brigade. It was so cold it wouldn't take long to get frostbitten. We had to sleep under the tanks. I remember one time my feet were totally frozen, and I thought I was going to lose my toes.

Part of my Intelligence training was to learn how to use spy devices, and sometimes we had to crawl down very small holes in the ground that were covered up and undetectable using monitoring devices that read and sent codes to headquarters. The devices could detect movement both in the air and on ground.

Overall, Germany was a good assignment. But eventually my time was up, and I was on my way to Vietnam. Uncle Sam gave me two months leave and be with my family friends before being shipped off to Nam.

When I got home, there was lots of talk about Vietnam and how many troops were losing their lives, and many people were protesting the war. My girlfriend at the time was sad and didn't want me to go to Nam. I tried to break off our relationship before I left, as I didn't want her to be waiting and worrying about me. She refused to break it off, so I asked her to promise not to write me a "Dear John letter." Dear Johns were letters troops received from their girlfriends or wives while away from home informing them their relationship was over, mainly because she had started dating someone else. Many troops became depressed, and some couldn't handle the bad news, acting out in bad ways, even attempting suicide, and sometimes being successful in doing so.

My girlfriend, however, was faithful and wrote me every week—while I was in basic training, advanced training, Germany, and Vietnam.

Chapter 10

Back in Vietnam

I could not believe I was in so deep. I honestly didn't believe I was going to make it home alive. There was so much going on, sniper fire all the time and incoming missiles—and sometimes they were friendly fire. We went out early in the mornings to get to our location and try to recover communication equipment that had been left behind when the compound had been overrun by the enemy. We didn't know if we would make it back to our base, which was about five miles away, because it was a hot zone. We caught a lot of sniper fire, and it was a perfect location for the enemy to do great harm to us. We often had to call in for help and have helicopters come in and fly us out.

Often, American planes would fly right over us and release "Agent Orange," a deadly chemical. It just looked like orange rain falling from the sky, and we had no idea that, years later, we would be affected by it. Agent Orange was a mixture of herbicides used to defoliate the forest areas that might conceal Vietcong and North Vietnamese forces and destroy crops that might feed the enemy. Many of my friends and other Vietnam veterans have been directly impacted by Agent Orange, including myself.

Agent Orange

The Veteran's Administration has recognized certain cancers and other health problems as presumptive diseases associated with exposure to Agent Orange during military service. These include amyloid light-chain (AL) amyloidosis, a rare disease caused when an abnormal protein, amyloid, enters tissues or organs; bladder cancer, chronic B-cell leukemias; and chloracne, a skin condition that occurs soon after exposure. Others are diabetes mellitus type 2; Hodgkin's disease; hypothyroidism; ischemic heart disease; multiple myeloma; non-Hodgkin's lymphoma; parkinsonism and Parkinson's disease; peripheral neuropathy; early-onset porphyria cutanea tarda; prostate cancer; respiratory cancers, including lung cancer; and soft-tissue sarcomas.

The number of Vietnam veterans affected by the chemical Agent Orange is astonishing. Roughly three hundred thousand veterans have died from Agent Orange exposure. That number is almost five times as many as the fifty-eight thousand who died in combat in Vietnam.

My story

The base we were housed in and worked from was also under constant attack from the enemy. After a few weeks, we got orders to go into Qui Nhon, which had just been overrun by VC (Vietcong) Vietnam Communists and the guerrilla force that supported the North Vietnamese Army, which fought against South Vietnam. We had to travel through a place called Death Valley to get there. With mountains on one side and a river on the other, it was a perfect place for ambushes. We made several trips in and out of Qui Nhon; each time, you just prayed to make it through.

We never hit any roadside bombs, but we took lots of sniper fire. Back at the base in Phu Thi, one night a sapper (North Vietnamese soldier) got into our compound with explosives.

Another night, we were trying to sleep, and we heard a big explosion outside the compound, so we went to see what had happened. A two-ton truck that was bringing water to us hit a roadside bomb and turned over. The driver and his shotgun rider were injured. I immediately grabbed my M16 and started low crawling toward them. A couple of my buddies were right behind me. Snipers were trying to pick us off, but we made it to them and secured the area. We waited for the medivac helicopter crew to get to us, which took about fifteen minutes or so; it wasn't safe, but they landed anyway. My homeboy from Washington, DC, was there keeping us covered also. The Medivac team was in and out in less than five minutes. I felt so badly for the two who were injured. They were just doing their job, trying to get water to us.

The brother I held in my arms kept asking me if he was going to die. I told him repeatedly that he was going to make it. When the medics got to him, he didn't want to let me go; he held on to me tightly. He felt comfort hearing my voice. The medics moved quickly because they were afraid of getting shot down; they just got the two of them on the helicopter as swiftly as they could and were out of there. I wanted to go with him. I think if I could have stayed with him, he would be alive today. Unfortunately, he didn't make it.

After about two months, our mission was over, and we returned to our home base down south in Long Binh. It was party time. We celebrated hard for about a week straight. I had developed some medical problems with my skin, arms, legs, and feet. It was hard to keep your feet dry during monsoon season, as it would rain for months at a time nonstop. I was given some ointment and blue pills to soak my feet in twice a day. I had this terrible itch, and I felt like my skin was crawling with bugs. The skin between my toes were raw. The treatment gave me some relief after a couple of days.

I spent the next couple of weeks trying to process all that had happened. I never in my life thought I would experience what I'd gone through. Death was more real to me than ever before, as it was constantly knocking on the door. The past couple of months had been tough for us, and I'd only been in country for a couple of months.

When we went out on our first mission, there were only two

teams in our unit, and we were team two. Now our unit had about five teams, but we didn't get to see each other, except for very short periods of time. Team one had been back from its first mission and was on its way back out again. We felt like we were more experienced than any of the other teams and shared some of our experiences with each other. Team one had seen just as much action as we had, but they were farther up north, closer to the DMZ. Fighting up north was more intense because you were fighting the North Vietnamese Army, who were highly trained, rather than Charlie (VC), who were the guerrilla fighters from the south.

One evening when I was taking a shower, one of the guys from team one was intentionally trying to frighten one of the new guys who was just getting ready to go out in the field for the first time. We were all taking a shower, and he went on and on about how horrible things are in the field. Even though he was right, I didn't like what he was doing. So we got into a fight. I was called into the captain's office the next morning and had to explain what had happened. To my surprise, he gave me a break, and I wasn't court-martialed or given an Article 15, which is simply a different avenue for handling a case.

It wasn't long before we were put on alert that we'd be shipping out within the week. We had no idea what our mission was or where we'd be going. As we were waiting for our security clearance, we learned the type of pay we'd be getting. When it all came down to it, we would be getting paid big-time. We all had to get top secret clearance, and not the regular secret clearances, and we would be getting three types of pay—regular pay, TDY (travel duty pay), and hazardous duty pay. When we picked up our orders, we were excited—we were going to Thailand. We thought this must be a mistake, as there wasn't any fighting in Thailand.

Chapter 11

Thailand

We made our way to Thailand. We had to take several flights, one on a small twin-engine plane just big enough to carry our small team. That was a scary flight. While we were flying, we suddenly heard this loud noise coming from the right engine. It choked out and then started back up, only to choke out again. We were instructed to prepare for a crash landing. We were told to get all sharp objects away from us. We were a little less than halfway to our destination, so the pilot decided to return to our departing location. We had a fifty-fifty chance of making it back, but it wasn't looking good for us. I remember once again praying to God for His help. Well, we did make it back to that base. We were shaken up, our lives flashing right in front of our eyes.

We were told to board another plane right away and took off again. About two flights later, we finally arrived in Thailand. When we got to the airport, we were picked up by a military transportation team and taken to a really nice place called the Windsor Hotel, in Bangkok, Thailand's capital. We couldn't believe we'd be staying at this nice hotel. Not even twenty-four hours ago, we'd been in the jungles of Vietnam taking cold showers and going to outhouses to use the bathroom. Now we were in civilization, with hot water and toilets that flushed, clean white sheets on real beds, and private rooms. We felt like we were in heaven.

A week later, we were called into our first briefing to go over our first mission and all the details. Our first assignment was to go to a place called Takhli in northern Thailand to do some security work. We had US troops fighting in Laos and Cambodia along the Ho Chi Minh trail. This was the route that sent weapons, manpower, ammunition, and other supplies from communist-led North Vietnam to their supporters in South Vietnam. Our job was to support those units with intelligence and reestablish communications, as well as to help the navy battleships at sea get proper radio signals from those units on the ground and from radio towers so they could give them artillery support during battle. This was a highly classified and dangerous mission, but after what we'd been through in Vietnam, this sounded like a walk in the park—at least that's what we thought.

We had to wear civilian clothes and blend in with the other troops who were on R&R, military slang for rest and relaxation or rest and recreation. Many troops came to Thailand for mini vacations. For security reasons, we changed into our military gear and left the hotel early in the mornings around 0300 hours (3:00 a.m.) and came back around the same time so we didn't bring attention to ourselves.

We completed about four missions without any casualties, but we received a lot of sniper fire on some occasions. We were working close to the Burma, Vietnam, Cambodia, and Laos's borders, which was very dangerous. On two of the missions, we had to climb five hundred-foot antennas to adjust the disks to new latitude, longitude, and elevation settings. The enemy snipers would try to knock us off as we climbed up the towers. Once we were out of their range, we were safe, but as you climbed down, the snipers would be ready to take you out. So we had to learn how to maneuver and move rapidly. Our own sniper team did a great job protecting us as we moved up, down, and around those towers.

We would toss coins between ourselves to decide which two would be going up the antennas. The enemy sniper had to be good to hit us because, as we climbed the antenna, it would be swaying back and forward, not making us an easy target. I remember hearing the shots from the snipers, but only once did a round hit close to me. I heard the bullet hit the antenna and ricochet off, and that only made me move faster.

On one mission, one of our guys was pinned down by sniper fire on his way down, and he stop moving at the halfway point. This was a bad place to stop because you were in range of the sniper. After our team cleared the way for him to completely descend, he was paralyzed with fear, so I had to go up and get him. When I got to him, I thought he'd been shot, but he was just afraid to move. He was one of our best and could move like a monkey on the antennas. But this day, he was in deep, and there was more than one sniper shooting at him. Timing was everything, so I looked him straight in the eyes and said, "We are coming off this towel alive. On the count of three." We moved with dispatch and made if off. When we got off the tower, he was so grateful I'd come to his rescue.

Some of our missions were to do reconnaissance, which is a military observation of a region to locate enemy activity. We would take pictures and gather other intelligence.

After each mission, we'd return to Bangkok and regrouped. It was strange to be out in the boonies one day and then sleeping in a nice clean bed in a hotel, taking a nice hot shower, eating well, and enjoying all kinds of entertainment the next day.

The Windsor Hotel was nice, with several dining rooms and clubs and kickboxing every evening for our enjoyment. There were beautiful theaters, restaurants, and massage parlors. Every establishment had a picture of the king and queen on the walls in full view. Thailand is known for silk, and there was a tailor's shop next to the hotel that would make clothes and shoes. I had a couple of nice silk shirts made. We saw the Buddhist monks every day walking around. And whenever we went out to the countryside, it was beautiful, and we would see these amazing large Buddhist statues in the mountains.

Our next to last mission was a bad one. A small team like ours was attacked at night while sleeping in one of the local villages in a place called Phitsanulok. I'm not sure what their mission was, but things went totally wrong for them. I assume they were doing recon missions in Laos, which was very close to that location. They came under attack and had great casualties.

We had to go in and try to gather any information related to the attack, and we could feel the overwhelming spirit of death in that place when we got there. We got there midday and were given a briefing. We had three local villages to cover to gather information pertaining to the attack. These little villages were like something you would see in a martial arts movie. It was normal to see a group of people having gang fights in the middle of dirt roads with swords and knives and martial arts. It was like being in ancient times.

We weren't allowed to use firearms; we could only engage in hand-to-hand combat with knives and machetes if we had to defend ourselves. On this mission, we couldn't wear military uniforms so we wore other clothing, like jeans and sweat shirts. I had a long machete strapped over my shoulder with a black bandana wrapped around my head, and I wasn't supposed to carry my .45 pistol, but I hid it in my back sack.

We were all angry about what had happened to our comrades and wanted to get even. Our job was to question the locals and try to figure out who had done this terrible thing to our troops. We did get into one big fight with some of the locals that evening as we went through the villages. I took a unique set of knives away from one of the guys I was engaged in fighting with. I kept the set as a souvenir.

We were exhausted from everything we'd experienced that day but so wired up we didn't even attempt to sleep. We stayed on high alert for the rest of the night and were picked up early the next morning. We all felt very sad over what had happened to that team and that we couldn't really get any helpful information.

I didn't sleep well for the next couple of days afterwards and noticed I had to have a few drinks before I could doze off to sleep. I was beginning to have terrible nightmares.

The last few days in Thailand were interesting. We were told when we first got in country that we couldn't get involved with any of the women, and we knew to never talk to anyone about our missions. We had to be extra careful with the women, as some of them were informants for the enemy.

However, after our first mission, we all ended up taking up time with some of the local women just to have fun and hang out with them to pass time. It was nothing serious for us, and we never gave them our real names or talked about what we did, even though I knew they were curious, as we would disappear for weeks at a time.

We only had a couple of days left in Thailand at this time, and we tried to avoid the women all together. But the last night I went to the club next door to the hotel to have a drink, and one of the women came up to me. She looked upset. "Napoleon," she said (it was my alias), "come outside. I want to talk to you."

I went outside, and she walked away from me towards the darker area alongside the club. Her head was hanging down, and I couldn't see her hands. I thought something was wrong. She turned around, and her hands were behind her back. I knew right away she had a knife and wanted to harm me.

"When are you leaving Thailand?" she asked.

I responded with a sincere tone voice, "Not for a long time."

"You're lying to me," she said. "You're leaving tomorrow." And she started walking towards me with the knife in her right hand.

I had to make a quick decision—try to get away from her or talk her down. I decided to try to reason with her. I was able to get the knife away from her and talk her down. I was trying to figure out how she knew we were leaving. Later, I found out one of team members who was hooked on one of the other women had sold us out.

Chapter 12

Back to Vietnam

Going back to Vietnam was depressing. I kept thinking about the good and bad experiences in Thailand. If I had a choice, I would have preferred not to return to Vietnam. I'd enjoyed the nightlife and good food, sleeping in a nice clean bed, and taking a nice hot shower. Even our missions weren't as bad as being in Vietnam.

I only had a few months left on my tour of duty in Vietnam; time was going swiftly. I'd done and seen much in a very short period. I was thinking more and more about going home, and I didn't want to go back out in the field in Vietnam anymore. I had a very bad feeling. The fear of getting killed that had overwhelmed me when I'd first arrived in Vietnam was back.

There was a lot of talk that the enemy from up north was making its way south, overrunning other American compounds. I knew this firsthand because, in Thailand, we could see how the North Vietnamese were making their way south, using trails in Laos and Cambodia.

Our government was slowly trying to withdraw American troops from Vietnam but, at the same time, leaving some areas vulnerable to the advancing enemy. I didn't want to go back out in the field, because it was too dangerous; the odds of making it back were slim to none. However, I would be loyal to my team. I remember praying to God, "Please keep me alive. And if I have to go out again and I get shot, just don't let me lose my private parts or get shot in the head." Anything else, I thought at the time, I could survive.

Some of the other teams were out on assignments, and when they came in, they looked beaten down and discouraged. Things were getting bad. We started getting assignments with the combat engineers who we shared the same compound with. We had members from the 101st Air Borne, 1st Calvary, and the Korean Marine Corps. We all worked together on different missions.

Casualties in Vietnam

I was in the US Army, and we had the most fatalities of all the branches of the military in Vietnam. The Department of Defense database shows that, of the 2,100,000 men and women who served in Vietnam, 58,152 were killed. The army suffered the most total casualties, 38,179, or 2.7 percent of its force. The Marine Corps lost 14,836, or 5 percent of its own men. The navy fatalities were 2,566 or 2 percent.

Of those killed, 997 soldiers were killed on their first day in Vietnam, and 1,448 were killed on their last scheduled day in Vietnam. The life expectancy of a door gunner was about two weeks. One out of every ten Americans who served in Vietnam was a casualty. A total of 300,000 black Americans served in Vietnam. Among the roughly 11,000 American women stationed in Vietnam, Sharon Lane was the only one killed by hostile fire. Seven other women died in accidents and illnesses.

My story

A few months later, I was considered a short-timer, which meant my orders to go home could come in at any time. Everyone called me Bro Pop, and for some reason, I was the person they came to for advice. All short-timers could carry a short-timer's stick, which was a customized stick. Some were like walking canes or half that size in different colors. I was happy to get my short-timer's stick, which was black and about three feet long, with a black fist on the end. I had engraved on both sides of my boonie hat "Blackness." I guess that's how I was feeling about the war in Vietnam, and how brothers were being treated.

I just wanted to make it home alive and see my family and friends again. The brothers always talked about getting back to the world, the United States, to see our beautiful black women and to protect them. We called them sister me's, which meant we are all one in the spirit, and as black men, we were obligated to take care of them.

Finally, one day my orders came in. My team had just received orders to go back out in the field. They were all glad for me. I was excited about going home, but I felt bad for them; I knew it was going to be a tough mission for them. As I was packing, my team was getting ready to go out. I said my goodbyes, gave up the dap for the last time to the brothers, and gave a hung and peace sign to my white brothers. The reality was we were all brothers, trying to survive one day at a time.

There were three places we could depart from Vietnam—Tan Son Nhut Air Base in Saigon; Cam Rahn Base in Cam Rahn; or Da Nang Air Base in Da Nang, which was up north. I was sent to Tan Son Nhut Air Base in Saigon, which was near my home base in Ben Hoa. When I got there, many troops were waiting to catch a flight out of Vietnam. The air base was under constant attacked with rockets and mortars—just like it had been when I'd first arrived in Vietnam in Cam Rahn Bay.

Commercial aircrafts, which we called the freedom birds, had a hard time landing because of the attacks. Once the aircraft landed, we had to move with dispatch, as they didn't have much time to get us aboard and take off before the next attack.

I remember sitting in that waiting area right off the airstrip waiting for my freedom bird to land. I could see it coming in from a distance. As it got closer, the landing gears came down as it was about to approach the short runway. It was an American Airline plane. I was getting excited, and my heart rate increased as I watched it get closer. In a matter of seconds, that excitement went away. The sirens went off, indicating incoming rounds again. I watched as the landing gears went back in and the plane went back up into the sky. We ran for cover. It was like just coming in country all over again. A few motor rounds came in, but it wasn't as bad for me, as I'd been in plenty of air attacks by now and survived them.

The airfields were always a hot place. Finally, after about three days, we were able to get a flight out. I remember like it was yesterday. As we boarded the plane, we were all so incredibly quiet you could hear a pin drop. The flight attendants were all brave middle-aged women who kept a positive attitude, but you could see the urgency on their faces. The plane engine started, and the tension and anticipation deepened. Suddenly, we were moving down the runway. As we lifted into the air, total joy broke loose. Everyone was shouting in loud voices thanking God and just feeling grateful to be going home.

Back then, you could smoke on the planes, so we smoked our cigarettes, and the flight attendants served us miniature bottles of alcohol. And yes, we all got wasted on that fight back home.

I remember thinking, *What just happened?* I thought about all those who were still in country, while I was on my way back to the world (as we called the United States). I thought about my team who'd just gotten new orders and were on their way back in the field. Some of them were short –timers as well. I just prayed to God they would make it home safely. I prayed for all our troops in Vietnam and all the innocent civilian Vietnamese men, women, and children. War is hard, and the civilians suffered as much as those who were fighting.

Chapter 13

Back to the World: Home from Vietnam

We finally arrived at Oakland California Air Base after a long flight. I can't remember if we stopped at other locations on the way back to the United States. When I got off the plane in Oakland, many of the troops fell down and kissed the ground. I was thinking this was just one big dream. Had I just had this amazing experience? Obviously, it wasn't just a dream, and I had really gone to war and back. Things were quiet at the base. I didn't hear any of the familiar sounds or smells. No helicopters flew in the sky. No firearms went off in the distance. There wasn't the smell of marijuana or of the burning of body waste. No brothers were getting together dapping. Things felt different. I had been in the jungles of Vietnam only a few hours, ago and now I was back in the United States.

As we were processed back into country and went through a debriefing, I couldn't stop thinking about my team in Vietnam and what they must be going through. We had to go through medical examinations and be cleared before we could go home to see our families.

I was still having problems with my skin and feet and was given medications to take. I was glad to be home, but I felt out of place at the same time. I remember being anxious and unable to sleep in the barracks, as it was too quiet. I zoomed in on every little noise I heard.

While in Vietnam, I didn't get much sleep at all. I had gotten use to catnapping and always being on hyper alert. . I was now lying in my bunk in the barracks that were safe, clean, and quiet, and all I could do was stare at the ceilings, unable to sleep. Some of the guys went out in the town of Oakland to party at the bars, but I didn't want to hang out. I just wanted to go home.

After I finished totally processing in and was getting ready to get orders for my new unit before I went home on leave, the clerk asked me if I was interested in getting out of the service now because of a new bill that had just been passed by President Nixon. The bill stated that any soldier coming home from Vietnam with less than six months left to serve could be honorably discharged and get credit for those months. This sounded like a great idea to me, as I had less than six months left on enlistment. I asked the clerk if he was joking. He said he was serious. Without a second thought, I said to him, "Absolutely, I'm interested."

This worked out well for me. After all I'd gone through in Vietnam; all the politics involved in the war; and the fact that so many lives were lost, some due to political reasons, I was full anger. I was happy to get my discharge orders and be released from the military a few days later.

I was able to get a military standby flight from Oakland, California, to Washington, DC. When I arrived at the airport I, called my girlfriend to let her know I was home from Nam and to pick me up if she could. She was able to come and get me right away. We were happy to see each other. She was a nice person, and we had a special connection. But when I'd joined the military and had to leave home, I'd pleaded with her to break off our relationship. She'd refused to, so we'd stayed together. We wrote to each other on a regular basis during my entire time in the military.

When I was home on leave from Germany on my way to Vietnam, I'd had a conversation with her about Dear John letters. I told her that, if she ever decided to see someone else, I would rather get the Dear John letter while in Vietnam than to come home and find out. After all, we both were still young and to ask her to put her life on hold for three years wasn't fair to her. She never admitted she was with anyone while I was away. Some of my friends made allegations in letters while I was in Nam, but I never took them seriously.

She picked me up at the National Airport in Washington, DC, which has since been renamed Ronald Reagan National Airport. We were excited to see each other and decided to spend some private time together before I did any visiting to see family and friends. It felt good to be home, and I was trying hard to put Vietnam out of my mind, but it just wouldn't go away. Most of my days were spent thinking about all the things I'd been through. I was trying very hard to readjust to civilian life and move forward. I felt a dark cloud over my head, and my thoughts about Vietnam became uncontrollable. I didn't want to be around people, and my girlfriend noticed right away that I'd changed. I wasn't into drugs, but I would drink beers and sometimes hard alcohol. I was still having a hard time sleeping, and sometimes I would drink more to help with sleeping. The times when I would fall off to sleep, I would have terrible nightmares about Vietnam; I'd wake up totally saturated in sweat. My dreams were so real I felt like I was back in Vietnam.

I had been living with my brother Walter and his family when I'd enlisted. When I got home, though, they were living in a much smaller apartment and had a new addition to the family, my niece Arlette. So I went to live with Uncle Clifford and his family. He was my father's oldest and only brother and was living in Maryland right outside of Washington, DC. While I was in the service, I'd been sending my uncle government bonds and some money through an automatic allotment so I would have some money when I got home.

The first thing I wanted to do was get a car. So, my uncle took me to Sheehy Ford dealership in Marlow Heights Maryland. I saw a beautiful 1972 maroon Buick Grand Sport 455, and I had to have it. My uncle signed for the loan, as I didn't have any credit or a job at the time. I made the payments directly to my uncle, until I was able to get a job and get my name put on the loan.

This car was a beast, and I loved it. Imagine I am straight out of Vietnam, a little wild, and now I have this hot car. My first cousins who I was living with were loving to me. They knew I was having a hard time readjusting, but they never judged me for being a little wild.

They loved to sing together as a group and would practice almost every day. I watched them develop over the years. There was my cousin Ronnie, who to this day has his own band (and they're great); my darling niece Veronica "Pookie"; Marreatta "Bay"; and Chris. I only stayed with them for a short period of time before I moved.

My buddy Irving had gotten home from Vietnam about six months before I did and got married to my girlfriend's first cousin Wannie while I was still in Vietnam. I was happy for them. They were really in love with each other and made a perfect couple. So, the four of us would spend a lot of time together just hanging out and having fun.

There were only a couple of people I felt comfortable talking to about Vietnam, and that was Irving and my friend Jeff, both of whom had served in Vietnam and could understand what I was going through; they had some of the same issues going on in their lives. Irving and I spent a lot of time together sharing Nam stories, drinking beers, and just hanging out. He was a door gunner and crew chief with the 101st Airborne and had gone through a lot also. It was therapeutic for both of us to be able to talk about what was on our minds. Most people didn't understand us and what we'd experienced as Vietnam veterans.

I loved Irving's entire family. They were like my second family. I spent a great deal of time with them. They were all full of life, and we laughed together a lot. Tony was the youngest brother; Gwen, the oldest sister; Baby Sis was next; and then came Doll, Nina, Sheena, and the baby Yoshie.

We all liked to go to parties, and back then, we had plenty of house parties with the blue lights in the basements. We'd listen to the Chi-Lites, Marvin Gaye, Peaches and Herb, and the Delfonics along with Earth, Wind and Fire and the Unifics, just to name a few. Those were the good old songs and real lyrics.

I got a job in an apprenticeship program to become an electrician. I was working at the Fort Meade Army Barracks, wiring the new barracks. I stayed to myself most of the time. One day while we were taking a lunch break, I was sitting alone close to the woods on a log eating my lunch. A helicopter flew overhead and I had my real first flashback. It was scary; for about a full minute, I was back in Vietnam, hearing the Vietnamese talking. It happened fast, and it was incredibly real. When I came out of it, I couldn't believe what had just happened. I walked out of the woods looking back, trying to figure out what had just happened to me. The more I thought about it that day, I finally realized it was the sight and sound of the helicopter over my head and being in the woods that had triggered the flashback. It was one of many flashbacks to come.

Another time I was walking on the sidewalk with my girlfriend to visit my cousins. As we got close to the house, a truck was going down the street and backfired. I jumped into the hedges for cover, leaving her standing there. She looked down at me like I was insane. Once I realized it was only the truck backfiring, I felt embarrassed and just got up and brushed my clothes off. The same thing happened again when the local fire department siren when off as they were getting ready to respond to an emergency call. I left her standing in place while I jumped behind a car for cover.

My first Fourth of July home from Vietnam was overwhelming for me. I felt like a chicken with its head cut off, constantly ducking every time I heard firecrackers or explosions go off. Most of my friends and strangers looked at me almost like they were making fun of me. I was angry, as I didn't have any control over my mental and physical reactions to the outbursts or loud explosions that constantly reminded me of combat in Vietnam. All my friends loved going down to the Washington Monument to watch the fireworks display every year, and this year was no exception. Even though I would have preferred to stay home, I decided to go, which was a big mistake. I didn't like being around crowds anymore, and I surely didn't do well around the fireworks. That night, I ended up leaving everyone before the fireworks were over. I just couldn't take it any longer.

I didn't complete the apprenticeship program; the fifty miles each way were too far to travel daily, not to mention the expense for gas. I eventually just stopped going and looked for another job.

Eventually, my girlfriend and I decided to separate for a while. It was a very sad time for both of us, but it was necessary. We tried very hard to make it work, but it was too difficult for us to handle the ups and downs of our relationship at that time. I was changing more and more each day for the worse.

My world was getting darker. I would barely open myself up to talk with her about what was going on in my head. Most of the time, I was being haunted by Vietnam and would often just want to isolate myself from her and everyone else. I became very good at hiding my emotions and keeping everything inside.

The separation was tough. It didn't help my situation or hers. I started to drink more. She ended up dating another guy, and they got married after about a year.

Jeff was my other buddy from Vietnam. We'd served in the same unit and had gone on one mission together. We didn't have a lot of combat experience together, except for that one mission. We stayed in touch with each other and became even closer over time. One day we were hanging out, and he introduced me to his baby sister. We ended up going out on a date, and it went very well.

Jeff's family liked me because he'd talked about me and how I'd help him stay alive on that shared mission. I got close with all his brothers and sisters. They had a large family also. There were five boys and three girls.

One evening, Irving and his wife and I went to pick up my new girlfriend. They lived outside of DC in a place called Indian Head, Maryland. I was driving my car, the hot-rod Grand Sport car down 210 Highway headed back to DC. We were all feeling good having a few beers, blasting the music. Then I decided to pass a car in front of me that was moving too slowly for me. I floored the accelerator, and my car too off like a flashing light. As soon as I got around that car, I saw another car in the other lane coming directly toward me. I had to get back into the right lane to avoid a head-on collision. I was running about ninety miles an hour but was able to get back into the right lane to avoid a crash. But to my surprise, there was another car in that lane moving slowly. All I could do was try to slow down my car. I was doing well, and I thought I would be able to stop. But at the speed I was driving, I didn't have much room or time to brake all the way down. I barely hit the other car in the rear. The impact wasn't hard, so I thought the damage would be minimal. I got out of my car and rushed to assess. To my surprise, while the other car only had a minor dent on the rear bumper, the entire front of my car was totaled.

I was grateful to God no one was hurt, and the other car really hadn't sustained any damage. I couldn't believe what had just happened. The frame on my car wasn't bent, so I was able to get it repaired.

About six months after the accident, my new girlfriend and I decided to move into our first apartment together in Eastover, Maryland right outside of southeast Washington, DC on Audrey Lane.

I was working as a route salesman for a linen company. It was a hard job delivering linen and towels to restaurants, country clubs, and other businesses. It was very physically demanding, but I was able to do it with ease after a couple of months. I would cover over a hundred miles of territory each day, making anywhere between twenty-five and thirty stops. I learned the DC metropolitan area, along with southern Maryland and northern Virginia very well.

Everything was happening quickly for me. I got home from Vietnam in February 1972. Now it was close to the end of 1972, and I was living with my new girlfriend. We planned to get married on February 3, 1973.

I was still having terrible nightmares almost every night. My new wife to be saw how progressive my condition was getting. She'd witnessed the nightmares firsthand and was there for me when I would jump up in the bed terrified and soaked in sweat. She would hold me and tell me it was going to be OK. We would have to get up sometimes and change the pillowcases and sometimes the sheets. She was a good woman and was very supportive. I was suffering from PTSD and didn't know it.

The same nightmare haunted me for years. I had other nightmares, but this one was the worse. I was a prisoner of war, and I was on my knees with about five other comrades in a little place that looked like a tin garage. We all had our hands tied behind our backs and were on our knees. I was in the back of everyone else, and I could see the Vietcong soldier looking down at us with a handgun in his right hand. He walked up to the first GI, said a few words in Vietnamese, and then pointed the pistol point-blank at his head and pulled the trigger.

Then the Vietcong looked directly at me with a mischievous grin on his face. He would repeat the process with the next person and so on until he got to me. I was there on my knees after watching everyone else get executed. Now it was my turn to die. I would be trembling, looking only at his boots, afraid to look up into his face. I could feel the barrel of the pistol against my forehead and waited for him to pull the trigger. There would be a long period of silence as I faced death by execution.

Right when I thought he was going to pull the trigger I would wake up shaking, sweating, and terrified. I would be shaken up and angry but, at the same time, happy it was only a dream. But it was so real. Each time I would have that dream, it would take something out of me. This same dream would happen over and over for years. Even to this day, that demon will come back like it was yesterday, only to terrify me and to remind me he will never go away. It took me a long time to understand why I was having this terrible repeated dream. One day, it started to make sense because of something that had happened to me while I was in Vietnam—something I'd never talked to anyone about.

Back in Vietnam

When I was in Vietnam, we were in a place called Nha Trang, and we were allowed to go into the village to eat and have drinks. But there was a curfew. We had to be out of the village before dark. This one evening, I'd had too much to drink and didn't realize it had gotten dark and everyone had gone back to the base. This village was known to have Vietcong come in at night; the possibility of our being captured or killed was why we had to be out before dark.

I was still sitting in the club that evening as dark was approaching when one of the young Vietnamese women came to me and said with panic in her voice that a VC is in the village, and I needed to get out fast. But it was too late. I had no way of getting out. Everyone with transportation had left, and even if I'd tried to get back to the compound, it would have been dark, and I would have broken curfew and probably would have gotten into big trouble.

I sobered up quickly and asked her if there was any place I could hide, telling her I would gladly pay her for helping me. So, she sneaked me to her place and hid me in a little closet. There were about three other women in this little house, so I was at their mercy. I squatted in the tiny closet for about an hour before one of them came and got me. She led be by the hand and took me to another little house connected to that one.

They moved me several times that night until, around midnight, one of them came and told me I had to come out. The VC knew I was there, and one of the VC was her relative; he'd promised not to harm me, but I must do whatever I was told to do.

So, I came out. They were all sitting around a fire pit eating and drinking. All had their weapons lying next to them. They were drunk and speaking rapidly in Vietnamese and laughing. I looked around and did a quick assessment as I was slowing walking out to meet them, making sure my hands were in clear sight so that they would know I didn't have a weapon. I thought, *There're only six. Maybe I could take them all out if I could get to one of their weapons.*

They all had AK-47s, powerful Russian-made weapons. The only problem was I'd never used that type of weapon; one mistake on my part, and it would have been over for me.

Then one of them said to me as I walked out trembling, "Soul brother number 1."

I immediately repeated after him, "Yes, Soul brother number 1."

They all laughed and said some things in Vietnamese I didn't understand. I thought, *This is it; either they're going to kill me, or I'll be a POW.* Then one of them motioned for me to sit down.

I sat down with them. I could tell they were all wasted. The leader of the crew gave me a bottle with a dead bird in it with rotten eggs and some type of liquid; I think they called it rice wine. I took a swig of it, and it burned going down.

They laughed at me again and said, "Soul brother number 1." They passed the jug of wine around, and before long I was drunk with them. I just started talking trash and laughing and they were laughing. And then they said, "Soul Brother boocoo dinky dow," which meant *dizzy in the head.* This went on for hours, and all I could do was pray they didn't turn on me. I was face-to-face with the enemy drinking and getting drunk with them.

My insides were turning. I thought about the many times we'd fought against each other. I didn't know how this was going to turn out, but I had to stay calm and not lose my head if I wanted to survive.

It was a long night. I hung in there with them all night until the break of day, and they didn't harm me or take me in as a POW. Everyone had passed out by morning. But I still had my senses and knew that, once they sobered up, it could be trouble for me. So I got one of the women to take me to one of the Cyclos boys, a form of transportation used to get around in Vietnam, like a taxi service we use here in the United States, or the rides you can get on the boardwalk of Atlantic City, in New Jersey. She was able get me to one who was willing to hide me in the back and take me to the base, where I had to try and fit in with everyone else leaving the post at that time so I wouldn't get in trouble for staying out overnight and breaking curfew.

It all worked out. I was able to blend in with everyone and make it into the compound and back to my team. They were worried about me but didn't tell our team leader I wasn't there that night.

Chapter 14

It was getting close to our wedding day, and my girlfriend and I were both excited. I picked the date, February 3, to memorialize my mother, who'd passed away on February 3 when I was young.

When I was in Vietnam, I would pray to God that, if he got me through this war, I would get married and hopefully have a family to love and take care of. I would ask Him to please bless me with a son that could teach and raise to be a God-fearing man. I didn't realize my wife to be was already expecting our first son to be born in July. She told me about two weeks before our wedding day. I was shocked and filled with joy. She was about three months pregnant, so our son was conceived in October or November 1972.

We planned a large wedding with a guest list of well over two hundred people. My father traveled from Welaka, Florida, along with one of our good friends Rudy, who is the father of Patricia's, my sister's firstborn son, Rudy Jr. My sister was there from Florida as well. My uncle Clifford was happy to have my father there for the celebration. I knew once the two of them got together, the celebration would start early.

My wife to be and her oldest sister did most of the planning for the wedding and reception. We had a large wedding party, with six maids of honor and six groomsmen, along with a flower girl and boy and several ushers. Irving was my best man, and one of my bride's best friends from school was her maid of honor. We had the wedding ceremony in a large Methodist Church in northeast Washington, DC.

The night before the wedding, my friends gave me a big bachelor's party. One of my friends from basic training by the name of Hart hosted the party at his apartment in Washington, and we had a great time. I did the right thing and didn't get wasted. I didn't want to be hungover on my wedding day, so I retired from the party early.

The day of the wedding, February 3, 1973, I was only twenty-one years old, and my bride was just eighteen years old. We were so young. It was a cold, snowy day in DC, but it was a beautiful day as well. I thought about my mother, who'd passed away seven years prior. It was an honor to be dedicating this day to her as well.

As I stood at the altar with my best man Irving standing next to me waiting for my bride to walk down the aisle of the church to join me, I began to get nervous. I thought, *This is a big step that I'm taking, and I want to be a good husband and father.*

I looked out at everyone as they waited patiently for the ceremony to start. So many people were there from both sides of our families. I looked around to see if I could see my dad. There he was sitting next to my uncle Clifford. He was looking handsome in his tuxedo, and as our eyes connected with each other, he gave me a very proud smile. I was happy he and my brother and sister were there for the wedding.

I looked a little further and saw Ma Corley. She was looking beautiful and proud of me. For some reason, when I saw her, my nervousness went away. She always had a calming effect on me whenever I talked with her. She was a wise woman, and we had a deep spiritual connection.

Then suddenly everything snapped to attention. Everyone stood up as the front doors of the church opened and the organist began to play, "Here Comes the Bride." I looked with amazement in my eyes as my bride was being escorted by her father, the flower girl and boy leading the way, down the aisle to meet me so we could join as one. The ceremony wasn't long, and I was glad when it was over.

My new bride's sister who helped with the planning of the wedding and reception hosted the reception party at her home, right around the corner from the church. That worked out perfectly for everyone because of the snowy weather. June had a large, beautiful home, and she was the perfect hostess. We had a lovely reception party with lots of food and drinks and wedding gifts from our families and friends.

After the wedding was over, my dad and sister, along with Rudy, returned to Welaka, Florida, and we carried on with our lives.

Our son was born at Columbia Hospital for Women in Northwest Washington, DC, on July 29. I had requested to be in the delivery room when my son was born. So when my wife's water broke, we rushed to the hospital, and they took her into the delivery room right away and told me someone would come out and get me shortly. I was in the waiting room pacing back and forth, waiting to witness the birth of my first child. We didn't know if it would be a boy or girl. I did prefer for my first child to be a boy, as I had prayed and asked God for a son I could raise to be a good man. It was taking too long, and I was beginning to get concerned.

When the doctor finally came out, he said, "Congratulations, Mr. Gordon. You have a healthy baby boy." I was surprised and full of joy that it was a boy, and he was healthy. Though I was a little disappointed not to have been in the delivery room, but I was still excited that the two of them were OK and we had our first baby boy.

We named him Monzique Oscloropo Gordon. You may be asking why we picked that name. Well, I wanted to give my first son a unique name. So before he was born, I thought about it for a long time. One day while I was driving my truck making deliveries, it came to me. I was thinking about a name that would sound like my mother's name, Maurice. I took *Mau* in Maurice and changed it to *Mon* and changed *rice* to *zique* and came up with Monzique. His middle name, Oscloropo, is African and was given to me by my godmother.

I was proud to have a son, and I promised God I would take good care of him and raise him to be a good God-fearing man. I worked hard and did my best to keep my promise to God. Though I was still fighting those demons from Vietnam, I was determined not to give up.

One day when Monzique was around five years old, we noticed he was going to the bathroom a lot, but we didn't know what was going on. He slipped into a coma one evening, and we rushed him the DC General Hospital in northeastern DC, where he was diagnosed with juvenile diabetes and was in a diabetic coma for about a week. I remember standing over him as he lay in that hospital bed praying to God to bring by son out of the coma.

God heard my prayers and delivered him. I was elated the day I saw Monzique's eyes open. His mother and I were sitting in the room listening to the doctor's concerns that he may have sustained brain damage because of the coma's length. I was focusing on my son, and suddenly, his eyes opened. I shouted for joy. I jumped up and started talking to him, and he talked back to me and sounded normal. He asked us what had happened to him. The doctors took over and worked on him, and the next day he was doing much better and was able to eat.

Monzique had to stay in the hospital for about another week and had to learn how to give himself insulin shots twice a day and test his blood sugar levels. Before he could be discharged, I practiced with him using oranges, and he caught on quickly.

Within the next week, Monzique was released from the hospital. We all had to make some major adjustments in our lifestyles to make sure our son stayed healthy. His diet was very important, as were getting the proper exercise, taking his insulin on time, and making sure he tested his blood sugar levels. Eventually, Monzique got good at taking care of himself and getting to understand his body. He was in school, and it took some adjustments on his part, as he had to have snacks during the day and got special treatment from his teachers. That made him feel different from the rest of the kids, but he eventually moved passed those emotions and fit right in with everyone else.

I spent a lot of time talking with him to encourage him and to let him know this medical condition couldn't keep him from accomplishing whatever he put his mind to doing. I taught him how to play chess, and he caught on quickly. About a year later, he could beat me at the game. I was impressed with how good he'd gotten at only six years old.

God had also gifted him with the gift of arts. He loved to draw, and we noticed how good he was getting. My god brother Irving was a gifted artist as well, and he would spend time giving Monzique pointers.

One day, we were all at the mall in southern Maryland. One of the artists who would draw your portrait as you posed for him noticed how interested my son was, as he kept trying to interrupt the artist to ask him questions. The nice gentleman asked our son if he would like to draw a portrait with him and my son said yes. So he set Monzique up with the equipment, and they worked side by side. To our amazement, Monzique did very well with that picture. The artist was impressed and encouraged him to stay with it.

I was keeping my promise to God to be a good husband and father. I still wasn't getting much sleep, and the nightmares continued. We were fortunate to be able to move to a more upscale apartment complex in a nice neighborhood. I was working hard, and material things were coming fast—new car, money, and all the luxuries of life.

We were expecting our second child, and I wanted to make sure our growing family was financially secure. We were doing OK, as both my wife and I worked. Between the two of us, things were good, and we could keep up with all our financial obligations. But I got in my head and started to project negative outcomes. Like what would happen when she had to stop working after having the baby? Would I still be able to make ends meet? I was also thinking about my childhood experiences and how I'd suffered because of the hard times my parents went through. I thought of the nights I went to bed hungry and seeing our furniture set out on the streets. I remembered the promise I'd made to myself that I would never let my family go hungry or get evicted from their home.

So, I got this bright idea. I could make some money on the side by hustling—even though I knew it wasn't who I was and that type of lifestyle wasn't going to be healthy for me and went against all my values. However, I wouldn't listen to my conscience, which was telling me this was a bad idea. I made some contacts, and before long. I was in the game. I picked up some of my old habits that I'd developed while I was in the military—habits that didn't fit into civilian life. I started to be suspicious of everything and everybody. I had to watch my back everywhere I went and was always looking out for the police. I even started carrying a weapon again. Things escalated quickly. Before I knew it, I was in deep, living two separate lives. The hustling game was dangerous. But for some reason, I wasn't afraid. I thought that, if I could survive Vietnam, I could do anything.

The lifestyle continued, and things progressed. We started having big parties and going to concerts and living that lifestyle. We were young and naive. Our new lifestyle caused tension between us and in our marriage. We'd only been married for a very short time, and I was still having problems with the demons from Vietnam. Now I'd added more pressure getting involved in the hustling world.

One day, I got a call that my wife had to be rushed to the hospital because of complications with her pregnancy. She was only six months pregnant with our second son. Unfortunately, he was born premature and was put on life support because his lungs and other organs weren't fully developed. He only survived for about two weeks, and eventually we had to take him off life support. We were devastated. I wanted to give him a name so we could have a death certificate, so we named him Jesus Gordon.

Not long after the miscarriage, we decided to separate. It was a challenging time for both of us. She and Monzique stayed in the apartment, and I moved out. It was a dark time in our lives. I felt I had failed as a husband and father, and depression was knocking on my door.

Even though I was dealing with demons, I believed in Jesus Christ. I loved Him and knew He was still with me. I knew deep in my heart that I was a good person, and I never intentionally wanted to hurt anyone—physically, mentally, emotionally, or spiritually. I believed with all my heart that He would someday deliver me from those demons that had a stronghold on my life.

Chapter 15

After my wife and I separated, we remained friends and worked together to raise our son. It wasn't easy, but we put our differences aside and did what we had to do for him.

PTSD

PTSD wasn't really talked about back then. There weren't programs for Vietnam veterans to deal with PTSD. However, a few years later, I was introduced to a program for Vietnam veterans that was at the Vet Center on 8th and Pennsylvania Ave., Washington, D.C. It started out as a small group of about ten black Vietnam veterans. We met every Thursday evening at 8:00 p.m. We would sit in a circle with a counselor, and we all just made small talk in the beginning. The counselor didn't put any pressure on us to talk about Nam and would encourage us to come back the following week. Eventually, someone decided to let go and go in deep and talk about one of their experiences in Nam. After we broke the ice, eventually we all did the same, one by one. Some of us even broke down and cried. We built a bond with each other because we had empathy for one another.

I remember feeling anxious before each meeting. I would stand outside the meeting before it started and drink a cold beer before I would go in. It would take the edge off. We all still wore our jungle fatigues. People would look at me funny. I believe they thought I was a little weird. We were the lost veterans trying to find our way back home from the war.

The Department of Veterans Affairs estimated that between eleven and twenty out of every hundred veterans experience post-traumatic stress disorder (PTSD). It's a number that's both overwhelming and, unfortunately, not always acknowledged to the degree it should be.

PTSD is a mental illness that occurs after exposure to a traumatic event. Unable to cope with what has been experienced, the brain exists in a near constant state of fight-or-flight, with intense physical and emotional reactions triggered by memories of the event that are spurned by high-anxiety situations. For veterans returning from combat zones, the symptoms of PTSD often include nightmares, intrusive thoughts, and difficulties processing the emotions of the trauma. Other symptoms include difficulties sleeping and maintaining relationships, wild fluctuations in anger and aggression, and self-destructive behaviors.

My story

I was still working at the linen company. My job title was route salesman. I was good and fast. I was making good money, plus hustling on the side. I purchased a 1974 Grandville, white with burgundy interior. I put the gangster white wall tires on her, and she was smooth, with a big 400 engine with the four-barrel carburetor.

I was running hard, burning the candle at both ends. One day, I was unloading my truck and slipped off the tailgate and injured my spine. I had to go on workman's compensation. I was under the doctor's care for the pain and went to therapy about three times a week.

I couldn't work for about two years. I had to walk with a cane, and I wore a back brace. I believe this was God's way of slowing me down. One night, I was working a party making the money, and there was a guy at the party who was trying to outhustle me. Back then, if someone was having a house party, they would invite a hustler like myself to come and serve party favors to their guests. Anyway, the other hustler and I noticed each other and knew we were each other's competition. We decided to work together, as we both had good product. He was curious about my connections, and I was curious about his as well.

I had a bad reputation, but there was something about him I just couldn't figure out—until about two months later. He was an undercover narc (narcotics agent for the DC Police Department), but he was a dirty narc. Now I knew how he got his good product. So, I started running with him. We did a few jobs together. He was vicious and was well known in both the hustle and law enforcement worlds.

My alias was Pop, and I was well known also. We made a good team. I'm not proud of this time in my life, but that was my reality. We ran hard for several years.. On New Year's Eve of that year, we decided to get out of the game, and we did. I lot of things happened in the years that we ran hard.

I was cleared by my doctor after having a couple of medical procedures done on my back, and I'd received a settlement from worker's comp. So I decided to enroll in college and totally turn my life around. I attended Strayer Business College, studying to get my degree in accounting using my GI Bill. I made it through the first couple of semesters, but it was difficult for me to stay focused, so I dropped out.

A few months later, I started attending Prince George's Community College, studying psychology, and it was going well. I felt free from the hustling world but felt a little out of place because I was older than most of the students and was a Vietnam veteran.

I was still going to my Vietnam group meetings on Thursdays, and it was beginning to help me. The counselor advised me to go down to the OPM, which is the Office of Personnel Management and take the civil service exam. I took his advice and took the examination.

I was living up town in the Columbia Circle area of Washington,

D.C. with my new girlfriend. We were walking distance to the Malcolm X Park, the Meridian Hill Park that was officially opened in 1963. It became a gathering place for black activists. Professor and activist Angela Davis is often credited with publicly calling for renaming the park after Malcolm X in 1969, mirroring demands by local organizers like Jan Bailey of the Student Nonviolent Coordinating Committee to have a citywide holiday and a memorial in honor of Malcolm X. A 1970's congressional measure to rename the park for Malcolm X failed, but the name stuck.

Malcolm X

Malcolm X was born Malcolm Little on May 19, 1925, in Omaha, Nebraska. His mother was the national recording secretary for the Marcus Garvey Movement, which commanded millions of followers in the 1920s and 1930s. His father, a Baptist Minister and chapter president of the Universal Negro Improvement Association, appealed to President Hoover that Marcus Garvey was wrongfully arrested. His civil rights activism prompted death threats from the white supremacist organization Black Legion, forcing the family to relocate twice before Malcom's fourth birthday.

Regardless of the Littles efforts to elude the Legion, in 1929, their Lansing, Michigan, home was burned to the ground. Two years later, Malcom's father's body was found lying across the town's trolley tracks. His mother, Louise, suffered an emotional breakdown several years after the death of her husband and was committed to a mental institution. Her children were split up among various foster homes and orphanages.

Eventually, Malcolm and his buddy Malcolm "Shorty" Jarvis moved back to Boston. In 1946, they were arrested and convicted on burglary charges, and Malcom was sentenced to ten years in prison. He was paroled after serving seven years. Recalling his days in school, he used the time to further his education. He began to study the teachings of NOI leader Elijah Muhammad. By the time Malcolm was paroled in 1952, he was a devoted follower with the new surname "X."

Intelligent and articulate, Malcolm was appointed as minister and national spokesman for the Nation of Islam. He established mosques in cities such as Detroit, Michigan, and Harlem, New York. Malcolm utilized newspaper columns, as well as radio and television to communicate with NOI's message across the United States. His charisma, drive, and conviction attracted an astounding number of new members. Malcolm was largely credited with increasing membership in the NOI from five hundred in 1952 to thirty thousand in 1963.

Eventually because of some disagreements with Elijah Muhammad, Malcolm founded his own religious organization, the Muslim Mosque, Inc. He went on a pilgrimage to Mecca, Saudi Arabia. The trip proved life altering. For the first time, Malcolm shared his thoughts and beliefs with different cultures and found the response to be overwhelmingly positive. When he returned, Malcolm said he had met "blonde-haired, blued-eyed men I could call my brothers." He returned to the United States with a new outlook on integration and a new hope for the future. This time when Malcolm spoke, instead of just preaching to African Americans, he had a message for all races.

After Malcolm resigned his position in the Nation of Islam and renounced Elijah Muhammad, relations between the two became increasingly volatile.

After repeated attempts on his life, Malcolm rarely traveled anywhere without bodyguards. On February 14, 1965, the home where Malcolm; his wife, Betty; and their four daughters lived in East Elmhurst, New York, was firebombed. Luckily, the family escaped physical injury.

One week later, however, Malcolm's enemies were successful in their ruthless attempt. At a speaking engagement in Manhattan's Audubon Ballroom on February 21, 1965, three gunmen rushed Malcolm onstage. They shot him fifteen times at close range. The thirty-nine-year-old was pronounced dead on arrival at New York's Columbia Presbyterian Hospital.

Chapter 16

One day I got a call from the office of the Board for Correction of Naval Records, which was the highest court for the Department of the Navy. The call came from the executive director himself, Mr. John E. Corcoran Jr. I will never forget our conversation. He had a very stern but calm voice and said, "Is this Calvin C. Gordon?"

I said, "Yes, it is. Can I help you?"

"I've been trying to reach you for over a month," he told me. I have your military records on my desk, and I have a job opening for you if you're interested. If you are, you can start immediately."

This was around January 3 or 4, 1979, a year after I had stopped hustling. I asked what kind of job, and he said I want you to be my personal assistant. I didn't understand what the job entailed. But I said yes. He asked when I could start working, and I said on the fifteenth.

On the first day, I reported to a building in Alexandra, Virginia, called the Hoffman Building number two. There were two very tall buildings side by side, Hoffman I and Hoffman II.

When I got there, I was greeted by a nice young lady by the name of Vikki Taylor, who was the secretary for Executive Director Cochran. Vikki took me into his office to meet him. He was a very distinguished-looking middle-aged man with white hair. The first thing he asked me was about what I did in Vietnam. Even though I knew he had my military history and was aware of my background, I shared a few things with him. Then he asked how I was readjusting. I told him I was doing fair and had been attending the Vet Center's groups with other Vietnam veterans.

He shared with me that he'd already run a background check on me and that I'd been cleared for a secret clearance, which was needed for the job. "Your records also indicate you received a top secret clearance while in Vietnam," he added and went on to explain that I would be responsible for securing and transporting extremely sensitive information from several locations throughout Washington, DC, and Virginia, including the Pentagon and other civil service and military organizations.

Then he made a joke, saying, "No worries, you won't have to carry a weapon."

I just laughed. That was the icebreaker. I liked him right way, and I could tell he felt the same toward me. He was a retired navy rear admiral in charge of the highest military court for the Navy Department. He said he was impressed with my military records and the many commendations and citations I'd received.

The army was still interested in having me reenlist and become a trainer. I'd received several letters from President Nixon and other high military officials when I got home from Vietnam, but I wasn't interested in going back into the military as an instructor. He asked why I'd turned down the opportunity to be a special operations trainer for the army. I shared with him that I didn't like the politics of the war in Vietnam, how General Westmorland was treated, and that so many innocent American lives were lost. I noted how embarrassing it was for me and many other Vietnam veterans when South Vietnam fell to the Communists.

Watching the news on television, I'd been angry to the chaotic state at the American embassy in South Vietnam as the North Vietnamese Army took over.

The fall of South Vietnam

On April 30, 1975, the South Vietnamese capital of Saigon fell to the North Vietnamese Army, effectively ending the Vietnam War.

In the days before, US forces evacuated thousands of Americans and South Vietnamese. American diplomats were on the frontlines, organizing what would be the most ambitious helicopter evacuation in history.

The logistics of issuing visas and evacuating the Vietnamese and American citizens wasn't glamorous but was essential. American diplomats were behind every detail. Some diplomats showed exceptional bravery, saving Vietnamese citizens who would have faced persecution under the new regime.

Although the United States had withdrawn its military forces from Vietnam after the signing of the Paris Peace Accords in 1973, approximately five thousand Americans remained—including diplomats still working in the US embassy in Saigon. While President Nixon threatened a forceful response to a violation of the treaty, many factors, including lack of domestic support and the distraction of the Watergate scandal, provided an opportunity for the NVA to launch an offensive.

Throughout March and April 1975, the North Vietnamese Army captured more and more Southern cities. South Vietnamese citizens began to flee in mass numbers. The fall of the second-largest city, Da Nang, sparked even more refugees to depart.

On April 29, 1975, North Vietnamese troops shelled Saigon's Tan Son Nhut Air Base. US Ambassador Graham Martin ordered the evacuation of Saigon. By this point, sea lanes were blocked, and planes could not land in Saigon, leaving only one option for an evacuation—a helicopter airlift. After the compound was attacked, the US embassy became the sole departure point for helicopters. The original plans called to only evacuate Americans, but Ambassador Martin insisted on evacuating South Vietnamese government officials and the embassy's local staff.

Meanwhile, ten thousand South Vietnamese waited at the embassy gates, hoping to make it onto a helicopter. From April 29 to April 30, helicopters landed at ten-minute intervals in the embassy, including landing on the embassy roof. With some pilots flying for nineteen hours straight, over 7,000 people were evacuated, including 5,500 Vietnamese, in less than twenty-four hours.

My story

After my short meeting with Mr. Corcoran, he assigned a Marine to me who would teach me everything I would need to know. I would shadow him and be trained by him for the next month or so. He was a nice young man in his mid-twenties by the name of Roy. He was from Puerto Rico, stood about five foot seven and had dark hair and a warm smile. He always looked sharp in his Marine Corps uniform.

He took me around and introduced me to the entire staff, which was about ten attorneys and a few paralegals, along with legal and record clerks and, of course, the secretary Vikki, who seemed to be running everything. I was given a SAT security briefcase for transporting top secret documents and a special ID that stated I had authorization to carry documents in and out of the Pentagon, the State Department, and other governmental offices without being searched.

It was around 10:00 a.m. when Roy and I were out on our first assignment. We were on the tenth floor of the Hoffman II facing the large parking lot. I stood in front of a large window with Corporal Roy as he explained that Vikki had already called for a car and was given a three-digit number, which she had given to him. The civilian driver employed by the navy department would put three numbers on the dashboard of his vehicle when he arrived at our location. When we saw that number being displayed, we could go down, and the driver would take us wherever we needed to go. The driver would be assigned to us until we released him. Sometimes we went to more than one office to either pick up or deliver records and documents related to cases being tried in the military court. As I was standing there with Roy, our car came. I could see the numbers on the dashboard. He had his own briefcase, and I had mine. He had given me some documents and told me to lock them up in my case. Then he explained that I was to never let my briefcase out of my site or leave it unlocked.

We went down the elevator and got into the car. Our driver was a nice black guy who knew Roy well. "Where to?" he asked.

"The Pentagon, Mall entrance," Roy said.

There are five facade entrances to the pentagon, the Mall Terrace, the River Terrace, the Concourse, the South Parking, and the Heliport. So based on what office we were going to determine what entrance we would use. The pentagon is very large and complex. Within its halls are five concentric pentagonal rings, intersected by ten corridors, for a total walking distance of about 17.5 miles. So, the first thing Corporal Roy had to teach me was how to get around the Pentagon and all the different offices and titles of each department we did business with. The first office belonged to the secretary of the navy, because all cases had to be signed off by the secretary of the navy.

I felt especially important because a driver would pick us up and wait for us. We would go to different departments to pick up sensitive information on court cases and decisions from other boards members. We had investigators who gathered information for the cases that would be presented to our board, which was the highest board and made the final decisions.

I learned my job quickly and developed good relationships with all the different departments—DOD, the State Department, the Department of Veterans Affairs—and veterans organizations like the American Legion and Disabled American Veterans. I was entrusted with some of the most highly sensitive information. I didn't realize before I started working for the Board for Correction that the Marine Corps was under the Navy Department. There were many cases from both, their outcomes ranging from discharges up to court-martial and their subject matter ranging from rape and misconduct to AWOL (absent without official leave) but without intent to desert or desertion and many other types of legal cases.

After about a month of on-the-job training with Corporal Roy, I was on my own. Our office was taking on more cases and bringing in more employees and law students from George Washington University Law School, who were studying to take the bar examination.

About a year later, our office moved from the Hoffman Building in Alexandria, Virginia, to the Arlington Annex, which is considered an extension of the Pentagon. The two were within walking distance of each other. Also, it was the headquarters for the Marine Corps. Our office expanded very quickly, and the workload doubled in a short period of time.

I enjoyed my freedom—being able to move around and not have anyone looking over my shoulder and not having to sit at my desk all day. I knew my job well and took a lot of pride in making sure all the attorneys got the support they needed for their cases. They depended on me. And I had some good contacts, as I'd developed good relationships with the different department heads. So I was able to call and ask for favors on certain cases under their review for recommendations, to get them signed off as soon as possible.

Mr. Corcoran retired from the board and started his own law firm in DC. He told me he'd always have a place if I wanted to come with him. I decided to stay with the board.

Our new executive was a nice guy as well. Captain Pfeiffer was a naval retiree as well. He hired an office administrator by the name of Mr. Kessler. We didn't get along in the beginning because he didn't like the freedom I had. So he changed my job title and description to legal clerk and then to legal secretary. He hired two other people to help with my old duties, and I trained them both. They were nice people to work with their names were Ricky and Toni, who we are still good friends to this day. They learned quickly, and we all became close.

I was close with most of the Department of Navy drivers. They were all older men, veterans who always dressed nicely. They all took to me as well. We also had shuttles buses and vans that would run all day long from the Annex and Pentagon.

I had additional duties and had to learn how to type. To my surprise, I became a good typist. My new duties consisted of taking phone calls from petitioners and answering some of the basic questions they had concerning their situation and whether they qualified to apply to have their records reviewed. Once the application was received, I had to review it to make sure it was filled out correctly with all the necessary information. Once that was verified, I would order the petitioner's military records, either medical or administrative and sometimes both. Upon receiving the records, I'd assign the case to one of the attorneys based on the type of case and their workload.

Often the case workers, either the attorneys or law students, would need additional information as they were preparing the cases to present them to the board. So my additional duties included researching that information by referencing past cases. The Pentagon Law Library was our source to do that research.

It was still difficult for me to stay stationary for any long period of time, so staying busy working on cases was good for me. If I found myself getting up in my head about Vietnam, I would just get out of the office and walk or take a bus ride without anyone questioning me.

Our office building in the Arlington Annex was right next to Arlington Cemetery. If you walked out of the door, you could see the tombstones, which always reminded me of Vietnam and all the lives lost in the war. I was doing well, but every now and then, I'd have a bad day or week. One day, I was sitting at my desk, and the siren went off. I jumped under my desk. Just like that, I was back in Vietnam in my mind. My friend Toni, who was sitting at the desk in front of me, turned and saw me under the desk and told me everything was OK and I could get up. I felt embarrassed. She didn't judge me; instead, she showed me compassion.

One of the attorneys, Jack, who had been a medic in Vietnam had lost his right eye and lower left leg while trying to save another soldier's life in combat. We became good friends and got along well. At one of our office Christmas parties, we really tore on a big one and ended up leaving the party and hanging out all night in downtown DC. We ended up getting into some deep conversations about our experiences in Nam. He was truly an amazing person who didn't let his injuries keep him from moving forward in life. We both had the same demons haunting us.

Medics and radio operators in Vietnam didn't last too long. The life expectancy for him as a medic in a firefight in Vietnam was six seconds, and for me as a radio operator was about five to thirty seconds.

I decided to go back to school, so I started taking evening courses held at the Pentagon from Northern Community College. I needed to stay busy. So I would work during the day and then go to school at night. Then I got a second job working security on the weekends. Staying busy gave me less time to think about all I'd gone through in Vietnam and the street life.

I would still go to church and read the Bible but not on a regular basis. I got down on my knees and prayed to God every night before I went to bed and thanked him every morning for a new day. I was living in Arlington, Virginia, which was close to my job. I could walk there if I had to, which I did a few times, taking a shortcut through Arlington Cemetery. It was about a fifteen-minute walk. I had a nice apartment, and I enjoyed decorating it and making a wonderfully comfortable home for myself.

I was invited to a Vietnam veterans meeting trying to establish the first Vietnam Veterans of America Chapter. I went, and it was amazing to be around so many Vietnam veterans.

By the late 1970s, it was clear the established veterans' groups had failed to be a priority of the issues of concern to Vietnam veterans. As a result, a vacuum existed within the nation's legislative and public agenda. In January 1978, a small group of Vietnam veteran activists came to Washington, DC, searching for allies to support the creation of an advocacy organization devoted exclusively to the needs of Vietnam veterans. VVA, initially known as the Council of Vietnam Veterans began its work. At the end of its first year of operation in 1979, the total assets were $46,506. I paid my dues and became a lifetime member during that time.

Vietnam Veterans Memorial Dedication

Near the end of a weeklong national salute to Americans who served in the Vietnam War, the Vietnam Veterans Memorial was going to be dedicated. There was a march to the site by thousands of us. I had my son with me. Holding his hand as we joined the others, I felt the excitement in the air. It was November 13, 1982, and two days earlier, President Ronald Reagan had presided over the opening ceremony.

I still didn't like being around crowds, but this was different; these were my Vietnam brothers, and we had empathy for one another. On that day, a Saturday, Monzique, my son and I had packed a cooler with sandwiches, snacks, and drinks. We'd also packed a couple of blankets just in case we decided to stay overnight. I drove from Arlington, where I was living, to downtown DC and parked near the State Department, close to the new Vietnam Memorial site.

We left the cooler and blankets in the car and went to meet up with the other veterans in my group. We'd planned to meet at a certain place so we'd all be together. Monzique, who was nine years old at the time, would always hang out with me if I wasn't working. We made our way and connected with our group of about fifty to seventy-five Vietnam veterans. Some had family members with them too. It was a chilly day, and most of us were wearing jungle fatigues.

As we walked toward the memorial together lined up by twos, I held Monzique's hand. Every now and then, I noticed out of the corner of my eyes that he was looking up at me with great anticipation as to what was going to happen. The closer we got to the mall, the more my anxiety built. By the time we arrived at the site, there was a long line, and things were roped off to keep order. We waited patiently in the line, as it was moving very slowly.

After about an hour in line, we were close enough to see this long V-shaped black-granite wall. Inscribed on the wall were the names of the 57,939 Americans who'd died in the war, arranged in order of death. The designer of the memorial was Maya Lin, a Yale University architecture student who entered a nationwide competition to create a design for the monument. This was a powerful scene. In truth, the "wall" is made up of two identical walls that each stretch 246 feet and 9 inches.

When I got to the entrance of the memorial, I began to feel heavy with sadness and grief. There was a big directory in which you could look up names based on dates of death, telling you how to find those names on the wall. I located one of my buddies in the directory and thought about him and became sad. I could see the concern on my sons face when I tightened my hand grip on his hand as we started the walk down toward the cold valley of death. I could feel the spirit of death as we walked down looking at all the names on the walls.

Midway down, I stopped and searched for my friend's name. I couldn't find it. I kept on anxiously looking for his name. I wanted to give up, but I kept on looking until I finally saw it. Tears flowed down my face. I didn't think it would be so hard, but it took a lot out of me. Pearson was the only name I wanted to look up at the time. We had been in basic training together. There were others, like the guy who I'd held in my arms before he was airlifted and later died; I couldn't remember his name anyway.

People left flowers and other things on the ground in front of the names they found. Many just broke down and couldn't move for a long period of time. I felt like I was back in Vietnam. As we walked up on the other side gradually coming out of the valley, I was grieving for the first time.

I don't remember much more of that evening, except we all were crying and hugging each other, and the emotions were deep. I must have blacked out, as when I woke up it was morning, and my son was sitting up over me, just looking at me. I looked around and didn't remember much at all. I saw many veterans still sleeping. Tents were everywhere, and some were just getting their stuff together preparing to leave. When I came all the way back to my senses, the first thing I asked my son was whether he'd taken his insulin. He said he had, and all was good with him. So, we packed up and made our way home.

I talked to Monzique about this event recently, and he remembered it well. He shared with me that I was very hesitant to attend the gathering, but I pushed myself to go because the group of veterans I was associated with really wanted me to come. He remembers holding my hand as we walked down that long walkway and glancing up toward the wall. He said I was looking for a specific name and that I lifted him up to see if he could see it. He remembers us walking back to the car, getting the cooler and blankets, and going back to the mall. And he remembers hanging out with everyone all night, the veterans eating and drinking and even, in some cases, smoking pot. He said it got a little wild, and it was one big party. But no one was hurt, and I didn't do anything embarrassing.

Chapter 17

I thank God for my son. He had an incredibly challenging life. He was diagnosed with juvenile diabetes at the age of five. And when he started school, he found himself emotionally and physically challenged. He felt different from the other children in his class because he had to deal with the ups and downs of his energy levels impacted by the insulin in his blood. He was learning how to understand his body and to adjust to his new diet and lifestyle. Before he was diagnosed with diabetes, he loved to eat sweets, like most kids do. Now he couldn't enjoy eating the type of candy he'd been used to eating.

He would sneak and have candy every now and then. But most of the time he was good. He loved sports, especially gymnastics, which was even more challenging for him because it required a lot of energy. Sometimes, his blood sugar level would drop rapidly while he was exercising, and he would get very weak and have to stop. Once he learned he had to have a snack before exercising and to always keep a piece of candy on him in case of an emergency, he would have a candy bar to help bring his level back up. I usually made sure he had a Snickers bar on him as a backup. Once he learned his body's signals and knew when to adjust the insulin or take a snack when needed, he did very well.

I was one of his coaches when he joined a Little League basketball team. He used to get upset with me because I didn't show him favoritism. In the beginning, he just didn't have good coordination and ball control. His best friend at the time was John, who was very tall and big for his age. John was a pushover at first, until one day I helped him understand that he needed to use his weight and height to his advantage. He eventually caught on, and Monzique got better at handling the ball and became an incredibly good point guard. Even to this day, whenever he gets a chance, he loves to get me out on the basketball court.

Things were going well at the Navy Department, and my life was full. I was still attending school twice a week at the Pentagon and working a part-time security job at a large department store as a store detective. I was fortunate enough to move from my one-bedroom apartment into a nice three-bedroom house with a fully finished basement in Arlington, Virginia.

I was still trying to work my way up in the Navy Department and had hopes of becoming a federal investigator. Working two jobs and going to school began to take its toll on me. The store detective job was challenging and dangerous, as professional thieves would come in and rob the store. Sometimes, they had weapons, and if you tried to stop them, they would shoot at you out in the parking lot. I started carrying my handgun to work to defend myself if need arose.

One evening, I was on my way home from the security job and decided to take a detour and go downtown and have a drink at one of my favorite clubs. I had a few drinks and just hung out for about an hour and decided to make my way home.

On my way home, I had a collision with another car. We both failed to yield to each other as we merged onto Highway 295. When I got out of my car to see the damage, I forgot that I didn't have my jacket on. So my handgun, which was in my side holster, was showing. The driver of the other car just took off when he saw me. The police arrived as I was just standing there looking at the damage to my car. The officers pulled out their weapons when they saw my handgun and told me to place it on the ground. I did, easy, and lifted my hands in the air. One of them secured my weapon while the other kept his eyes on me. I told them I was a store detective and what had happened. I could tell one of them wanted to give me a break, but the other one wasn't going for it. I was arrested, as it was illegal to carry a weapon in Washington, DC, without a permit. My handgun was registered and legal for me to carry in the state of Virginia, but not in the District of Columbia. I ended up with my second weapons charge in DC, and I thought that I was probably going to end up doing some time in jail this time.

I had a big problem. If I was convicted and was given probation, which my lawyer thought would happen in this case, I would stand a chance of losing my security clearance with the federal government and probably be terminated from my job. Some strings were pulled on my behalf. I was able to beat the case, and the record was sealed, so I didn't lose my job or security clearance. But I decided to quit the security job. Once again, my prayers were answered. I was in deep trouble again; it was only God's amazing grace that saw me through that situation.

About six months later, I still wasn't advancing with the Navy Department and was feeling a little discouraged. I didn't enroll for another semester at school, so I decided to put in an application to become a correctional officer for the DC government. To my surprise, my application was accepted. When I got the letter of acceptance, I got nervous and started to have second thoughts. I had two weeks to accept or decline the position. A good friend who worked in law enforcement with the DC government counseled that, if I accepted the position, it would be like being in prison. With my personality type, he wouldn't recommend that field of work; he didn't think I'd last long and predicted I'd end up being miserable. So, after long consideration on my part, I decided not to take the job. I'm glad I didn't. The more I thought about it, the more I realized that, especially with my PTSD, I might have ended up in a worse mental state and may have ended up getting injured or hurting someone.

A few months later, I felt a great urge to make a career change. I thought it through and decided I wanted to go into business for myself, so I resigned from the Navy Department.

I bought a used Dodge van, which was perfect to start my

own courier business. The courier industry was big business in Washington, DC, because of all the private and governmental businesses that needed courier services. So, I stepped out on faith when I paid cash for the vehicle and then started looking for a way into that business. I searched through want ads and found a company from Canada that was new to the area and looking for individuals to partner with as private contractors. I went downtown and interviewed with the company, and everything worked out. I started my business about a week later.

Since I had a van, I was able to get contracts with companies that delivered office supplies and computers. This worked to my advantage, as the other new contractors had only cars or motorcycles. I could easily fit computers, typewriters, and other office equipment in my van.

I was satisfied with the short-term contract with this Canadian company. I was responsible for paying my own taxes and keeping my books, and the money was looking good. I was making twice as much as I had working with the Navy Department and security put together.

A new computer company that had started operations in the DC metropolitan area and had big contracts with the government and many law firms in the area needed my services daily. So I was contracted out to them for about six months straight.

The computer world was just beginning to take off, and the company kept me busy Monday through Friday. Everyone was buying computers, printers, and electric typewriters. I developed good relationships with most of the computer technicians who worked with the company and would go the offices and set up the computers after I delivered them.

I learned how to set up the computers, so when they got there, all they had to do was load the software and run analysis. This cut down on the time they had to spend with each client, allowing them to be more productive. The company was very pleased with my service, and they had a captive market, so business was booming.

The owners liked the work I was doing, especially helping the technicians get set up. To my surprise, one day, the one of owner asked me to stay at one of the weekly Friday staff meetings to discuss productivity and strategies and to recognize the top salespersons of the week.

This company was growing so fast it was getting harder for me to keep up with all the work. At the meeting, the owners, who were engaged to be married soon, asked if I was interested in coming on as a full-time employee instead of being a private contractor. They offered me a salary that was hard to turn down. So I accepted the offer, starting a new chapter in my life.

About a month later, the company purchased a new Ford Econoline van and gave me a gas card to go with it. I thought they wanted me to leave the vehicle at the job at the end of each day. But that wasn't the case, I kept the van twenty-four hours. This was perfect timing, as my van was on its last leg.

I enjoyed the work I was doing and the freedom of not having to be in an office setting all day. The company was right on the cutting edge of the new technology, with computers, printers, and networking systems doing extremely well. I got along with everyone, and we were like one big family.

The owners invited me to their wedding. I was truly honored by the invitation. The wedding, the most eloquent I'd ever attended, was held at a beautiful place on the harbor in Baltimore, Maryland. He was from Newfoundland, and she was Jewish. It was a very interesting ceremony, mingling both Jewish and Christian customs. It was two wedding ceremonies in one.

I moved downtown, which was closer to my new job. I was renting from a very nice woman from Brooklyn, New York, who was now living in DC. She was a retired American Airline stewardess and a smart businesswoman. She was buying old zombie homes in the Northwest area for about a hundred dollars and then renovating them and selling them and making a great profit.

I had some experience with painting, so one day she asked if

I'd be interested in helping her whenever I had some free time. I accepted her invitation and made time to help her whenever I could because she was a nice person.

My life was full, working with the computer company during the day and painting in the evenings. The computer company was growing so rapidly the company had to expand to a larger location and eventually had to secure another location in Fairfax, Virginia. I was able to get Toni's father a job working part-time in the warehouse. Mr. Talbert was a nice man who lived in the same neighborhood I'd grown up in as a young man. He was retired from the post office and was just looking for part-time work, so it worked out well for him. Toni and I worked together at the Navy Department.

After about two years, the company called an emergency meeting. We were informed the owners had decided to sell the company. At this point, my future was uncertain. I didn't know if the new owners would keep me on or if they already had their own staff. It turns out they gave us two-week notices, and that was the end for us. I was terribly upset and felt betrayed, but it was totally out of my hands.

I had no idea what I was going to do. But I did have a little money in my savings account and could collected unemployment for a few weeks. I continued helping my good friend with the houses, and that lasted for about two years. We must have renovated five homes during that time; it was a lot of work, but it paid off.

I was also getting frustrated with my life and began to wonder if leaving the Navy Department had been such a good idea. Or maybe I should have taken that position with the Department of Corrections. Things were not looking good for me, and I felt like depression was knocking on my door once again.

I had stopped going to the Vietnam groups because we'd all graduated from the program and received certificates of completion. There were other groups, but I didn't pursue them. The readjustment program for Vietnam veterans, a new program, only lasted for about a year for each member. I also noticed that my drinking was getting heavier, and my life was becoming unmanageable. I was beginning to isolate again, and the dreams about Vietnam were coming more often. I even had thoughts about going back to the old world and lifestyle I'd been deep into back in the '70s. I decided I needed to get away before I made that unwise decision again. I thought about going to Florida, where I could get a reprieve from the stress of life I was experiencing. So I called my dad and explained what was going on. He gladly invited me to come and stay with him for as long as I wanted to.

Monzique was doing well in junior high school. His mother and her new husband were starting their family together, and they were all happy and doing well. It took me about three weeks to get everything in order as far as selling my furniture and other things I'd no longer need.

Then I had to face my son and give him the unpleasant news about me leaving—a conversation I dreaded. I went to visit him, and we sat down and had a nice long conversation. He understood. I was honest with him about what was going on in my life, and I wanted him to know that I would never abandon him; he could come and visit me during the summer after school. I knew we'd miss each other because we always spent quality time together, no matter how busy I'd gotten. Even though I felt guilty for making this hard decision, I knew it was the best thing for me to do at that time.

Chapter 18

I took a train to Florida, and my dad picked me up at the train station in Palatka. We were glad to see each other. I hadn't seen him for a couple of years, and he was getting up in age but still had rather good health. He was still driving and working.

It was like starting life all over again. I loved the little town of Welaka, where I'd once lived when I was very young. It was nice to get away from the city life so I could do some desperately needed soul searching. I got settled in with my dad, and he was happy to have me with him. He loved the fact that I liked to cook and enjoyed the meals I'd prepared for us.

It didn't take me long to get an automobile because I was still getting my unemployment benefits, and I had a little money saved up. I was able to get a job working at this company that delivered ferns, used by florists as decoration for floral arrangements. It was very physical work. We loaded several tractor trailers nightly with these plants. It was a little degrading to me, but I humbled myself, as there weren't many job opportunities in this small town and its surrounding area. I really didn't know how long I was going to stay there.

I was still young, but time wasn't on my side. I was confused about what I wanted to do with my life at this point. I knew it wasn't going to be in this small town; though I loved the serenity, there wasn't a bright future for me there. I was working at night and sleeping during the day. I didn't have much of a social life except going to my aunt's café where everyone hung out and played pool or cards, danced, and drank. It was the only hang out spot in Welaka.

I had other friends who lived in Jacksonville Beach, about an hour away. I'd kept in contact with some of them over the years, and I'd visit every now and then, whenever I just felt like getting away from Welaka.

I was getting bored and came to accept that I needed to move on with my life. I found myself getting depressed and feeling empty inside. I thought about my life and wondered, *How did I end up like this?* There had to be a purpose for my life. I just needed to find out what it was and pursue it.

So, I got another bright idea. I would go and work with my cousin and her husband in North Carolina. My dad understood how I was feeling and wanted me to be happy and have a fulfilled life, so I went to North Carolina. My cousin and her husband ran a migrant farm workers camp. Yes, unbelievably, I'd gone from hustling after Vietnam to working for the federal government to owning my own business to now working on a farm as a cook and keeper for the camp workers. The latter didn't last long; I quickly wearied of babysitting grown men.

One day, my cousins asked me to drive up to New York City and find a few guys who wanted to work and bring them back to the camp in North Carolina. I took one of the guys from the camp with me, so we only had room for three or four guys. On our way to New York City, we had a few beers. I was stopped by the New Jersey Highway Patrol for driving too slowly. When the officer asked for my driver's license, I asked him to give me a break, noting that I was a Vietnam veteran. He was a little sympathetic and said, if he ran a check on me and everything came back clean, he would let me go. When he ran my driver's license, it came up suspended. I was arrested and was given two tickets and told I would get a court date in the mail. I wasn't able to drive because I had unpaid tickets, so the police kept my license. The guy who was riding with me had to take the wheel until we got to New York City.

Once there, we went to a spot in Manhattan were many guys just hung out looking for work. It wasn't a place I wanted to hang around for long. I got out of the car and talked to some of them, offering them a job in North Carolina working on a farm. Some of guys looked at me like I must be kidding, but a couple were desperate. I could tell they wanted to get off the streets of New York. Three of them decided to take me up on the offer. Two wanted time to go and get some of their belongings, but I told them, if they wanted to go with us, they had to leave with us now. They all looked homeless, hungry, and tired. They got in the car, and we didn't waste any time getting out of New York. They all had a terrible smell, and we kept all the windows down. In New Jersey, we stopped at a diner and brought them breakfast and then made our way back to North Carolina.

My job was to run the camp and keep everything in order. So, I cooked breakfast and dinner for about twenty men. There were two men to a room, and I had to make sure they kept their rooms clean. I had my own private room until we got a new guy, and I had to let him share a room with me. I wasn't happy about it, but I had no choice. He was a nice, quiet older guy. But we had one problem. He snored very loudly, and that was a big problem for me. I was still having problems with sleeping. I would average maybe four of five hours of sleep a night, and sometimes I'd get no sleep at all. After about two weeks dealing with this guy and not sleeping, I was stressed out.

Eventually all these issues were getting the best of me. I wasn't getting much sleep, and my attitude was getting bad. I was having Vietnam dreams almost every night, and they'd worsened to the point I didn't want to sleep.

I thought it would be a good idea to have my son visit for a weekend, since we hadn't seen each other in some time. His mother put him on a bus, and I picked him at the bus terminal. We were happy to see each other, and I was hoping to just have a good weekend with him.

Unfortunately, things didn't turn out as planned. The guys were getting on my nerves that weekend. I didn't want anyone coming to me to ask for anything. This weekend was supposed to be for me and my son. I told everyone to go and see my cousin if they needed anything.

My cousin and her husband secured a private trailer for Monzique and me for that weekend. There wasn't much for us to do, but we were happy to see each other. On Saturday evening, a couple of the guys kept knocking on my door interrupting my private time, and I got angry. I went over to the camp and got into a big fight with two of them that escalated into a big scene. I totally lost it and pretty much cleared out the entire camp. My cousin was upset. She and her husband got things under control about an hour later. The police were called, but no one was arrested.

I believe all the anger that had built up in me over the years came to a head, and I just exploded. I was done with everyone there at this point. All I wanted was out. So, the next day I put Monzique on the bus headed back to Washington DC. I packed up my car with my belongings and made my way back to Florida.

My car broke down about two hours into the drive. It ended up that I'd blown the engine and had to leave the car on the side of the road. I was able to get a ride from a couple of nice guys who were on their way to Florida.

When I got back to Florida, my dad had already heard about what had happened. He was a little disappointed in me, but he was a very compassionate man, so he didn't give me a hard time about it. My life was bad. I knew I needed to seek out some professional help.

Chapter 19

Back to New York

I was told about a VA medical center in a place called Northport, New York, that had a very successful program for Vietnam veterans suffering from PTSD. Veterans from all over were trying to get into this program, so I decided to make my way to New York to see if I could get in.

I packed up my things and headed out. The last time I'd made that trip from Florida to New York had been after the tragic passing of my mother, when I was only fifteen years old.

A friend in New York allowed me to stay with him until I could get into the program at the VA medical center.

I thought getting in the program would be an easy process, but it wasn't that simple. I had to go through a psychological evaluation first. Once I completed the screening, the program directors suggested I be admitted and observed for a few weeks before deciding whether the program would best suite my needs.

I was put on medication to address my sleep issues and the nightmares. To my surprise, I was sleeping well for the first time in many years. After a few weeks, I was accepted into the program, which would last three months. I was off the medication, and the groups were helping. The days were long, and everything was strict and organized.

I begin to feel some hope coming back into my life. Even though I would still have the nightmares about twice a week, I was learning to use the program's tools to cope with my fear, anger, resentment, and survivor's guilt.

During all the years prior to this program, I hadn't realized I was carrying around guilt because I'd survived the war, but some of my friends had not. The counselors, doctors, and staff members in this awesome program were great people who helped me and many other veterans get our lives together.

My entire hospital stay was about six months. During that time, my relationship with God grew stronger and I began to feel a sense of purpose for my life. Though I didn't know where I was going, I knew God had an awesome plan for my future.

I had about two weeks left in the program. Prior to being discharged, you had to have a discharge plan. I knew I didn't want to go back to my hometown, Washington, DC. Nor did I want to go back to Florida. Most of the veterans in the program were from Manhattan, Brooklyn, Queens, and the Bronx, so they had homes and some had jobs to go back to. I didn't have either. I was beginning to panic. But because my relationship with God had improved tremendously, I did what I knew to do. I prayed and asked God to show me what to do. It was as clear as day when He answered me. I followed His direction and went to the personnel department at that facility and put in an application for a job.

With only a week left in the program, I went to check on my application and learned there was a job opening for a supply clerk in the Acquisitions Material Management Service (AMMS). I interviewed for the position and was hired on the spot. I would start in two weeks.

AMMS was a small office of four people—the chief of the service, Mr. Brown; his secretary, Mrs. Monteverde; and the assistant chief, Mr. Andersen, whom I would work directly under. This service was responsible for all the supplies and contracts services for the entire hospital. The warehouse workers, purchasing agents, contract officers, and surgical supply department (SPD) all came under this office. It was a great job and a lot of responsibility.

Because of my previous service with the Navy Department and the time I'd already put in with the federal government, they had to offer me the same pay grade I'd been on when I'd resigned. This was great for me.

I had secured a job before my discharge date, but I didn't have a place to live. It turned out God had already worked that out for me. There was a temporary housing building on the grounds for the medical residents. I applied for it and was given favor. So now within two weeks, I had a new job and a place to live. I knew it was God working things out for me.

The medical center was a very large place. It was like going to a luxury country club, with a golf course, tennis courts, an Olympic-style swimming pool, and a very nice gymnasium. I couldn't ask for anything more.

I worked hard and eventually was promoted to secretary for the assistant chief. Mr. Andersen was a nice person to work for. He never gave me a hard time about anything. The chief, Mr. Brown, and I became good friends, along with Mrs. Monteverde.

The hospital was just beginning to become computerized. My previous experience with computers gave me some familiarity with the basics, and I was able to pick up new technology quickly. I became the ADPAC for our service, which meant I had additional duties, among them teaching others in our service how to use the computers, which were new to everyone. As the liaison between the computer center and my service, I was able to meet some of the individuals working in that department, like my good friend Charlie, who I call the master mind in the computer world. We were used to using typewriters and sending messages from service to service, but those days were coming to a halt.

About a year later, a computer assistant position opened in the computer center. I applied and was selected. Getting a job in information resource management (IRM) was a dream come true. This department was for highly educated individuals with degrees, and all I could do was thank God for favor.

Everything was going well for me. I moved from the temporary housing on the hospital grounds into my own apartment and was able to buy a car. I started attending another group for Vietnam veterans at the vet center in a town called Babylon. I was working and attending meetings, and life was getting better. Though I was still having problems with sleep and the dreams, it was manageable.

I enjoyed my new position and the increase in salary as well. Life was truly looking better, beyond my wildest dreams. I worked hard in my new position as a computer assistant alongside three others. We installed computer systems and printers throughout the entire hospital—all the units and services. I learned how to work with the systems department that maintained the mainframe and would come in once a week and back up the entire hospital system. Charlie and Kamil taught me a great deal about the systems functions, on which everything was totally reliant for the end user to function at all.

About a year later, a programmer position came available in the software department. I knew I didn't have the qualifications. You needed at least a bachelor's degree to be qualified as a programmer. But I was encouraged to apply anyway.

I applied for the position, and again God showed me favor. I was selected. The programing job was demanding, and I felt very challenged. I had to take courses and work at the same time, learning as I went along. I had to learn how to program in MUMPS (Massachusetts General Hospital Utility Multi-Programming System) or M, a high-performance transaction processing key–value database with integrated programming language. I had to take several courses and study awfully hard.

Only a few of us were supporting the entire hospital and keeping it up and running from a software perspective. It took about three years before you could really get a handle on things. I learned a great deal, and it really changed my life. I developed a passion for my new job and became particularly good at it, I must say. I started out supporting small packages. Eventually, I was assigned to bigger packages, like surgery, radiology, pharmacy, nursing, and lab. These where highly demanding packages to support.

I got to know many people at the hospital and became friends with many of them. I met a woman, and we started dating and eventually got married. She was a nice person, and we enjoyed each other's company. She had been married before also and had three other children. They were all in their teens and very nice and respectful. They were living in a home she and her ex-husband had lived in, so they sold their house, and we purchased our home in Massapequa, New York, and started our own family. I was a little hesitant about having another child, but I thought it would be nice to have a little girl to spoil, since I couldn't do that with my son, who was now in his late teens.

Ariel was born in September 1992. I'd prayed for a girl since I already had a boy. I was able to be in the delivery room when she came into this world. I was fortunate to be able to witness the entire process and took pictures of her birth—an amazing experience to capture. I had much respect for women who gave natural childbirth after I saw all the pain her mother went through bringing her into this world. She was born at Good Samaritan Hospital in Islip, New York. I remember how proud I was after the nurses cleaned her up and brought her back to her mother. I had one of the nurses take a picture of me giving my beautiful daughter, Ariel, her first rose.

Life went along pretty well for the next five years. Even though I was still having problems with sleep and the bad dreams of Vietnam, I refused to take the medication the doctors were recommending. Taking the meds interfered with my mental capacity, especially at work. So, I suffered through it all.

Life showed its ugly head when Anthony, my wife's oldest son, my stepson, who was living with us at the time in Massapequa, decided he needed a change and wanted to move to Richmond, Virginia, to live with his father. There was rising tension in our home related to curfews. Just weeks after he'd just moved to Virginia, we were awakened by the phone around 2:00 a.m. I didn't hear the conversation between his father and mother, but I knew in my spirit something was terribly wrong. She hung up the phone and started to weep and groan. Anthony had been shot in the back and killed. He'd gotten into a struggle with a guy who had a pistol. He'd been able to knock the weapon out of the guy's hands and continued to fight with him, but one of the guy's friends, a young man around sixteen years old, had picked up the handgun and shot him in the back.

This was a terrible hardship on the family. To witness a mother lose her son to murder was a breathtaking experience. I searched my heart for the words that would bring her comfort but could not find such words. We traveled back and forth to Richmond for the trial of the young man who'd committed the murder. There was a lot of tension between us and the family and friends of the young man. He was found guilty of second-degree murder.

Anthony's death also caused a lot of tension in our family, as some partially blamed me, believing I'd forced him to leave New York. That was not the case. However, I did feel guilty, as I'd been trying my best to be a good stepfather to Anthony. I hadn't wanted him to make the same mistakes I'd made. We had a good relationship, and he could identify with me as I could with him.

We began to have challenges in our marriage and decided to seek professional help. So, we went to counselling and continued to try to save our marriage. I decided to find a home church, in the hope it would help our marriage and family stay together during these tough times.

Chapter 20

I started attending the Hollywood Baptist Church, a well-known church in Amityville. The pastor, Andy C. Lewter, was an extremely popular preacher in New York. In fact, my wife and I had been married there, and he'd performed our marriage ceremony.

I learned a lot from Pastor Lewter, and eventually I was asked to join the deacon board. I also started teaching Sunday school for the intermediate boys. A few years later, I started a ministry called Boys to Men Young Brothers Ministry, which ministered to the young men in the church and community. I genuinely enjoy working with the young men and being a deacon. I learned a lot from my mentor, Deacon Fred Miley, who took the time to teach me much about the ministry.

Pastor Lewter was innovative, and as technology was changing, he wanted to keep up and use the latest to help the church. Once again, my background in computers was forefront, and I was able to help him.

My family had joined the church as well, and things were getting better. But as happens, the enemy got terribly busy and did whatever he could to bring about confusion and separation.

I got to know the pastor's family well, especially his wife, mother Ruth Fuller Lewter, and oldest daughter, Rosalyn. And I would get an opportunity to talk with their son Bishop Lewter, who was pastoring in Ohio. They had another daughter, who was the youngest child, Tonya, who I had never met.

Mother Lewter took a liking to me, and I liked her very much. Eventually, I grew to love the two of them. After my separation with

Ariel's mother, I had to take a break from Hollywood because there was a lot of tension.

Going through the divorce was tough, but we got through it. It wasn't easy on my daughter or myself or her mother. This was another dark time in my life. I really wanted to protect my daughter from the pain of a broken home. Ariel was only seven years old, and I never wanted her to feel like I'd abandoned her in anyway. I knew it would be best for her to stay in our home with her mother, so I sat down with her and did my best to share with her and explain what was going on, and she understood.

The time came when I had to start the process of looking for a place to live. I didn't want my daughter to think I was leaving her, so I told her she was going to have something more than her other friends—a nice big house *and* a nice apartment.

She was excited about that idea, so we went apartment hunting. It took us about two weeks to find the perfect place. It was out in eastern Long Island in a town called Patchogue—a spacious two-bedroom apartment with an indoor and outdoor pool, tennis and basketball court, and a nice dayroom.

The leasing agent was a kind woman. I explained my situation, and she appreciated me including my daughter in the plans and having her name put on the lease. I still remember the smile on my daughter's face when she picked up the pen and signed her name on the lease.

Then we went shopping for new furniture for our new apartment. She picked out her new furniture and helped me make decisions on the living and dining room furniture. It took us a few weeks to get the apartment fully furnished and decorated, and once we were done, it was a nice-looking apartment.

Ariel stayed enrolled in her school in Amityville, and her mother and I shared joint custody. She spent most of the weekdays with her mother and most weekends and the summer months with me. Times were difficult for all of us, but we made it through with the help of God.

My daughter, Ariel

In Ariel's freshman year, she started running track for Amityville High School. She became an exceptionally good runner and held records in the 100-, 200-, and 400-yard dash. And in the four-by-one and four-by-four relays, her team held records for Amityville High School until her senior year.

She went on to college and ran track for St. John University. As a proud dad, I was at most of her track meets cheering her and the team on. She also went to the Penn relays and other track events and achieved all-American at AAU Disney track and field.

She graduated from St. John's University with the class of 2014. After graduation, she wanted to take a break before pursuing her master's degree, so she got a job working for a day care center, which she always enjoyed. Even while she was in high school during the summer breaks, she would work at the day care center at the Northport VA Hospital, where she had gone as child. Ariel always talked about someday starting her own day care center.

After a few years at the daycare center, Ariel decided she wanted to start a family of her own. She married a genuinely nice young man named Gerald, and they started their own family. Their firstborn was Zara. The second was Amos, and he was a miracle baby. He weighed just one pound seven ounces, and the doctor's didn't expect him to make it. He had many surgeries and was in the hospital for about six months. God truly blessed him. The third was Abishai. So Ariel has given me one granddaughter, Zara, and two grandsons, Amos and Abishai.

Ariel is a great wife and mother to her husband and children. She has experienced her share of challenges as well. She was diagnosed with colon cancer a month before the pandemic broke out in 2020. She was blessed to be able to have a successful surgery to remove the cancer before the hospitals became overwhelmed with COVID-19 patients. She is cancer free today.

My son, Monzique Gordon

My son faced many challenges in his life and overcame them all. He was diagnosed as a juvenile diabetic at the tender age of five years old, but that didn't keep him from making the necessary adjustments to have a healthy life. He graduated from Lackey High School in Southern Maryland and attended Maryland University. After a couple of years in college, he decided to take a break, during which he pursued his lifelong dream of being a great artist. He worked hard and got better and better. He painted portraits of most of the family members, including several of me, my daughter, and other friends.

As time went on, he decided to add craft tattooing to his craft. To my amazement, he mastered it quickly. He was able to open his own tattoo shop and did extremely well.

Monzique is the father to three of my grandsons, Daniel, Darius, and Tadre, all of whom are very talented in their own ways. He is married to his lovely wife, Wanda, and they are raising a beautiful family together. In fact, in 2021, they were blessed with their first grandson, Pierre.

Monzique as touched many lives with his gift from God. It is amazing how blessed he is. Recently, one of my good friends Mr. Edward Bates, a World War II veteran, passed away at the age of ninety-five. I had the privilege of officiating over his homegoing service. I asked my son to bless the Bates family with a portrait of Mr. Bates and his wife, who had passed away a few years earlier.

My son blessed the family with two amazing portraits, one of Mr. Bates and another of him and his wife together. They have a lovely family, and his daughters, Dawn and Christina, whom I love dearly were impressed and thankful for the amazing work my son had done. Their entire family has an appreciation for art, as Mr. Bates was a great artist himself. In fact, Mr. Bates and I had conversations about my son's gift, and he offered to help Monzique in any way he could. Dawn, a college professor, has been extremely helpful to me on this project. I am truly grateful for her.

9/11

On September 11, 2001, I was on my way to work at the VA medical center in Northport, New York. Around 8:45 a.m., I was driving on the Southern State Parkway in Long Island, and I was running late. I was listening to the radio and heard that an American Airlines Boeing 767 had crashed into the North Tower of the World Trade Center in New York City. I thought it was only an accident and didn't think much more about it.

When I got to work, everyone was hysterical and talking about what had just happened. We didn't have a TV in our building, so we went to the main building in the hospital and watched as the news unfolded. Around 9:02 a.m., the second plane—United flight 175—hit the World Trade Center South Tower. As we watched, about fifty-six minutes after being hit, the South Tower collapsed around 9:59 a.m.

The collapse, which lasted ten seconds killed over eight hundred people, including first responders, inside the building and the surrounding area. I couldn't believe what I was seeing. Tower one collapsed at 10:28 a.m. At approximately 9:45 a.m., a third plane—American Airlines flight 77—circled over downtown Washington, DC, before crashing into the west side of the Pentagon military headquarters.

Meanwhile, a fourth California-bound plane—United flight 93—was hijacked about forty minutes after leaving Newark Liberty International Airport in New Jersey. Because the plane had been delayed in taking off, some of the passengers on board learned of what was happening via phone calls.

I had friends who lived in Queens and shared with me they could see people jumping out of the Twin Towers' windows. It was an incredibly sad day in our history. I personally didn't not know if it was going to be an all-out attack on America, and all I could think about was Vietnam and preparing myself for war. It was exceedingly difficult to imagine everything that had happened. I thought about my friends who worked in the Pentagon and those who worked near the World Trade Center.

The attacks caused the deaths of 2,996 people and injured more than 6,000 others, 2,606 in the World Trade Center and the surrounding area, 125 at the Pentagon, and 265 on the four planes. On this sad day, the spirit of darkness hung over America, and many of us wept.

The days that followed were extremely difficult for me. My sleep was disrupted. Everyone was putting American flags on their vehicles. I wished at the time I was back in the military so I could join our troops on their way to war. The United States launched an international military campaign, known as the war on terror, targeting extremist Islamic groups throughout the Middle East, Africa, and Asia.

During this dark time in our history, we went to war in the Middle East. I was wishing I could do something to help our country fight this war on terror. I would have considered reenlisting if it were offered to Vietnam veterans. I was still able to assist from another perspective. As a computer programmer for the Veterans Administration, I oversaw several medical software programs that helped veterans receiving medical treatment at the VA hospitals. It gave me great pride to be able to keep those programs up and running well.

Many troops coming home from the war were treated at our facility for a variety of injuries, ranging from head injuries to loss of limbs. Seeing many come home with mental issues I could relate to was deeply saddening.

As of February 2, 2021, 7,036 members of the United States military have been killed in Iraq and Afghanistan. More than 2,300

American service members have been killed in Afghanistan, and over 20,000 have been wounded since the conflict began.

The Department of Veterans Affairs released a report showing that at least 60,000 veterans died by suicide between 2008 and 2017, with little sign that the crisis is abating despite suicide prevention being the VA's top priority.

I had many friends who were physically and mentally affected by this attack. Cases of post-traumatic stress are common among 9/11 survivors and rescue workers. Respiratory problems, like asthma and lung inflammation, also developed at abnormal rates for those in and around the World Trade Center during and after the attacks.

A good friend of over thirty years was part of the rescue team, digging through the rubble day in and day out looking for survivors. He was later diagnosed with cancer but was treated and is doing well today. Eighteen people were rescued alive from the rubble. It took rescue and recovery teams nine months to clean up the 1.8 million tons of wreckage from the WTC site.

Another of my dear friends, a pastor, was at work in a building very close to the World Trade Center and had to walk out of the terrible situation. He shared that it had been very frightening; he had walked and walked until he was able to cross over the Brooklyn Bridge.

Despite everything going on in this world, even with a dark cloud lingering over the United States of America, I continue to work and did my absolute best to stay focused. As time went on, things got better.

My wife Tonya

Eventually I went back to my home church, Hollywood Baptist Church, in Amityville New York. I'd been away from for about a year because of the drama during my separation and divorce.

I met my wife Tonya at Lewter Scott Travel in Roosevelt, New

York. Mother Lewter, who'd owned and operated the travel agency for over thirty years, asked if I could stop by her office and help her with some problems she was having with the computers in the office. So, one evening after I was done with work, I went to see if I could assist her with the travel software. When I got there, Tonya was in the office helping her mother. She was sitting at one of the desks working on the computer. Mother asked her to explain to me what the problems were. I was pleasantly surprised to see her; I'd only saw her a few times when our churches visited each other on special occasions. She was married and was professional, and I could tell she was very intelligent.

As she explained the software issues, I couldn't help but notice how glamorous she was. I maintained focus and stayed professional, though it was hard to keep my eyes off her. I was able to make some repairs, but I had to make an appointment to come back the next day to finish, as I needed help from one of my coworkers. We returned the next day and finished up the work, and Mother Lewter and Tonya were happy.

Tonya lived in New Jersey with her husband, so I didn't see her but maybe one other time when Mother Lewter invited me to come to Lewter Scott Travel office to listen to a multilevel marketing presentation at which Tonya and her husband were the presenters. I'd already been involved in several multilevel businesses, and this one sounded interesting, so I joined.

About six months later, on a bright Sunday morning, I was sitting in church on the front row, where all the deacons sat together. I was the vice chairman of the deacon board at the time. Church service was just about to start, and as I happened to look to my right, I saw Mother Lewter and Tonya coming into the sanctuary. I was happy to see Tonya. It had been a while. It was a great service that day. Daddy Lewter and Bishop Lewter preached a tag-team sermon, and the Spirit of the Lord was powerful.

My divorce was final. And though I wasn't interested in getting seriously involved with anyone at that time, I felt like I could move on with my life. I wanted to stay focused on my career and the ministry.

The next Sunday, Tonya was back in church again. I was curious, but I wouldn't dare ask anyone about her, so I just left it alone. The following Sunday, I noticed she wasn't wearing her wedding ring and wondered if she was having marital problems. I considered how difficult it must be on her and her husband if it were the case, given that she was married to one of the most prominent pastors of one of the largest churches in the Bronx. I knew the church must love her as their first lady because of her loving personality.

Tonya had started to sing with the choir, and she had a lovely voice. I would sometimes just stare at her and not realize I was doing it. She captivated me, and I was trying not to be pulled into the captivation.

One Sunday she wasn't in service; it felt empty without her there, and I felt sad. Then the next Sunday, no Tonya. I assumed that whatever problems she may have had in her marriage had been worked out. A few more weeks went by, and then she was back in service sitting in the choir stand with the other choir members. I looked at her hand to see if she was wearing her wedding rings. I didn't see them, and I was happy.

Bishop Lewter was traveling between Ohio and New York where he was pastoring Oakley Baptist Church in Columbus and co-pastoring Hollywood in New York. We had a church trip from New York to Oakley Baptist Church to celebrate the bishop's pastoral anniversary, and during that trip, I had the opportunity to briefly speak to Tonya. We didn't get into any deep conversation, as she was busy coordinating the trip, which she did magnificently. I could tell she wanted to have a deeper conversation with me, but the timing was just not right.

When we got back to New York, we did have the opportunity to talk. She called me one day and asked if I could stop by Lewter Scott Travel, as she was having problems again with her computer. It wouldn't print documents for her. I went to the office, and for some reason, the computer was cooperating with her. Nevertheless, it gave us a chance to talk.

She shared that she was going through a divorce. And of course, being the gentleman I am, I offered my ears anytime she wanted to talk about anything. Besides, I was an expert, as I had just gone through a divorce myself.

As time went on, we became good friends, and I was there to listen to her and give her support. We would go out and have dinner or just meet at Starbucks and have coffee and desert and talk for hours. I shared that I'd been married twice. And since neither of my marriages had worked, I was done with marriage. I think she was so disappointed in her failed marriage that she felt the same way, so we remained friends for a long time. Eventually, her divorce was finalized, and now we both were free.

During those years, we grew closer. Things were getting serious between us. But marriage was something we both were hesitant about. Because of our religious beliefs, we had to keep everything decent and in order, which was becoming a challenge for both of us.

We decided to get married in 2012 and had a very small ceremony. We both had already had large weddings, so something small and intimate was what we wanted. Her brother Bishop, Andy Lewter, married us, and her father, Daddy Lewter, was our witness.

Tonya is an amazingly, brilliant woman. She started New Millennium Development Services, a 501(c)3 nonprofit organization on December 8, 1997. This organization is an economic development service for affordable housing. New Millennium works with the Town of Babylon's 72H Initiative that creates affordable housing opportunities for first-time income eligible individuals and families throughout Suffolk and Nassau Counties in New York.

I've had the opportunity to work with her as her project manager and was honored to have been able to assist in building two affordable homes for the organization. I worked with her on other projects as well. I now serve as a consultant, because of other demands and responsibilities I have in the ministries I serve in.

New Millennium has demonstrated a commitment to economic development through its production of the New York downstate region's largest procurement forum, Long Island Community and Economic Development Conference (LICEDC). This platform brings together more than a thousand attendees, among them minority- and women-owned businesses (MWBE) and service-disabled-veteran-owned businesses (SDVOBs), along with other certified businesses and buyers from government agencies and *Fortune* 500 companies to nonprofit organizations and small to major corporations.

Tonya is also the CEO of Li Vie Development Services and coauthor of *Coach*, a full life coaching guide.

President Barack Obama

Work was becoming stressful. Our staff was dwindling as coworkers retired, leaving positions unfulfilled and an increased workload. I had over thirty years of dedicated service with the federal government, and retirement was sounding like a good idea.

However, to my amazement something happened that year I'd never thought I would see in my lifetime. A black man was elected president of the United States of America. Barack Hussein Obama was born on August 4, 1961, in Honolulu Hawaii. He became the forty-fourth president of the United States, serving from 2009 to 2017 and was the first African American to hold the office. Before winning the presidency, Obama represented Illinois in the United States Senate from 2005 to 2008. He was the third African American to be elected to the body since the end of Reconstruction (1877). In 2009, he was awarded the Nobel Peace Prize "for his extraordinary efforts to strengthen international diplomacy and cooperation between peoples." Obama was sworn into office in the United States, in Washington, DC, on January 20, 2009.

"A new birth of freedom," a phrase from the Gettysburg address, served as the inaugural theme to commemorate the two hundredth anniversary of the birth year of Abraham Lincoln. In his speeches to the crowds, Obama referred to ideals expressed by Lincoln about renewal, continuity, and national unity, stressing the need for shared sacrifice and a new sense of responsibility to answer America's challenges at home and abroad. Obama and others paid homage to Lincoln in the form of tributes and references during several of the events, starting with a commemorative train tour from Philadelphia, Pennsylvania, to Washington, DC, on January 17, 2009.

The inaugural events held in Washington from January 18 to the 21, 2009, included concerts, a national day of community service on Martin Luther King Jr. Day, a swearing in ceremony, luncheon and parade, inaugural balls, and the interfaith inaugural prayer service. The presidential oath was administered by Supreme Court Chief Justice John Roberts to Obama during his swearing in ceremony on January 20. In additional to a larger than usual celebrity attendance, the presidential inaugural committee increased its outreach to ordinary citizens to encourage greater participation in inaugural events compared to recent past inaugurals. For the first time, the committee opened the entire length of the National Mall as the public viewing area for the swearing in ceremony, breaking with the tradition of past inaugurations. Moments before Obama was sworn in as the first black president, Aretha Franklin—queen of Soul and singer of civil rights anthems—gave a stunning live rendition of "My Country Tis of Thee."

My dad

My father was proud to see our first black president of the United States of America. He was getting older and was beginning to experience some health problems. He loved wearing his hats, and he proudly had Barrack Obama engraved on one of them.

My dad, Aaron Gordon, was born January 25, 1928, and passed

away on February 9, 2010, a year after Barrack Obama was elected president. He lived to be eighty-two years old. He had some medical complications from a stroke and never completely recovered. I was blessed to be able take a flight from New York to Florida and just spend a few days with him and give him a haircut. He loved for me to cut his hair. He was loved by many people. He was known by the name "Pretty Boy" to all in his hometown of Welaka, Florida.

He was a very handsome man even into his older age and had smile that would steal your heart. He was a quiet man with great wisdom. He had a medium brown skin complexion, a slim stature, and blue eyes. I'm certain his roots could be traced back to one of the many African tribes with other than brown or black eyes.

The many notable black celebrities with natural blue eyes include Rihanna, Tyra Banks, and Vanessa Williams, to name a few. Evidence of blue-eyed Africans also abounds throughout Africa, including in South Sudan, South Africa, Nigeria, and Uganda. My dad loved his grandchildren and great-grandchildren. From my sister, Patricia, his grandchildren are Rudy, Tywanda, and Troy. Great-grands are Rashad, Jerome, and Jordan. From my brother Walter, grands are Kevin and Arlette. From me, his grandchildren are Monzique and Ariel, and his great-grandchildren are Daniel, Darius, and Tadre and, from Ariel, Zara, Amos, and Abishai.

My story

After thirty-five years of dedicated service with the United States federal government, I decided it was time for retirement. On May 1, 2015, I retired from the VA medical center in Northport, New York, where I had worked as a computer programmer (IT specialist) with some amazing people. Our service, information resource management (IRM) was responsible for keeping the hospital's computerized system up and running in order to provide quality service to our veterans.

Keeping things running smoothly at the medical center was a challenging task. But even with a small staff compared to other VA hospitals, we did an exceptionally great job. I won't mention everyone, but there are a few I'll mention by name. First is my good friend Charles. He was my mentor, and when I first came to work in IRM service, he took the time to work with me and teach me much in the hardware and systems department. He was and still is one of the great minds in the IT profession. Then there are the two Lloyds, both very intelligent. In my section were the two Karens, Barbara, Mary Ellen, Rodney, Lou, and Mickey.

There were so many other people who became like family over the years, among them Nancy, Tamar, Haffesse, and Robert, who was our service chief.

I had many friends from other services in the hospital—radiology, pharmacy, lab, travel, social work, surgery, and many others—as I supported their software programs for years.

There was my dear friend Margaret, who I call Coach, and her amazing husband, Scott, who has an incredible life story. She talked me into running my first 5k race at the VA medical center to support our Veterans. I wasn't a runner, but it was a great way to get into shape, so I gave it a go, and it wasn't too bad. We eventually joined the Northport running club and ran many more races together. Finally, when I was sixty years old, she talked me into running the New York half marathon which was 13.1 miles. Marathon. We had run plenty of 4k and 5ks but never a marathon. It was very challenging, but we did it. It took me two hours and forty minutes to finish the race, and that was excellent for my age group.

Going into the ministry

I retired on May 1, 2015, and I was excited to be starting the next chapter of my life. In January of the same year, I'd received my calling to preach the Gospel. I ignored it, as I was happy serving as the chairman of the deacon board at my home church, where I'd been a member since 1993, and I wasn't sure it was a true calling from God.

I prayed and asked God to confirm my calling. He did, and I accepted it. I talked with my wife, Tonya, about it, and she supported me.

I preached my initial sermon in the same month of my retirement and enrolled in New Life School of Theology in Amityville under the leadership of Bishop Andy C. Lewter, who happens to be my brother-in-love and one of the greatest minds that I know. He is a historian, a theologian, and a graduate of Harvard University.

I was catechized and ordained two years later as an elder on May 27, 2017, at Hollywood Full Gospel Baptist Cathedral. At the catechism, I had to stand before a board of clergy and answer 201 questions, all of which, through God's grace, I got correct.

I was introduced to the Call Unto Me Ministry three years earlier in 2014 by my dear cousin Joan. I was on vacation in Florida when she gave me the number and asked me to join them in prayer. So, I joined them on a call one morning when I got back to New York. I was so impressed with the ministry and the powerful prayer warriors that I decided to become a member. I'd just started my own prayer line ministry in the same year, the Serenity prayer line, and I was just learning how to conduct a prayer line, so it was helpful to see how they ran their calls. The Serenity prayer is still going strong seven years later.

The founder of the Call Unto Me Ministry, Mother Gloria Womack, is one of the most loving persons you'll ever meet. She welcomed me with open arms and was excited to have another male join Pastor Ed Williams, who had been the only male for years. He taught Bible study every Saturday evening and was a great man of God. I was called to be the pastor of the Call Unto Me Ministry in 2018, after the passing of Pastor Ed Williams, who served faithfully for many years.

The members of this great ministry are truly a force in God's kingdom. The ministry—which meets through telephone conference calls Monday through Thursday, praying for the world and all and any situation you can imagine—has grown tremendously over the years. On Fridays, we're live on Church Talk Radio and have a preacher bless us with a word from God. Then on Saturday evenings, we have Bible study taught by me, Pastor Lawrence, and others as appointed by us. Our members are from many different states, from New York, Ohio, and Michigan to Indianapolis, DC, and Maryland to the Carolinas, Alabama, Georgia, Florida, and California, along with many other places I know I'm missing. I dare not try to start mentioning names, as I know I'll miss someone. But these are the most wonderful God-centered individuals who are totally committed to serving God, and I am pleased to serve as their pastor, along with my big brother Pastor Otis Lawrence.

I also started a men's ministry in 2018 called God's Men of Truth. We meet every Thursday evening to study the Bible together. We also have deep conversations on many topics that help us grow as men of God. We pray for each other and any concerns we may have. These are some of the most amazing men I've ever had the opportunity to fellowship with in my life. I truly enjoy serving with them. They include Brother Carney from New York; Brother Terrell from Atlanta, Georgia; Brother Bradley from Michigan; Brother Lawrence from California; and Sidney Brown from Long Island New York, along with my cousin Brother Dunn from Georgia, Brother Mark from California, and Brother Yinde from Georgia. There are many others who can't join on a regular basis because of other commitments.

As I've developed my preaching and teaching style over the years, several individuals have been very influential in my spiritual development. First was my father-in-love, Daddy Lewter, who has since gone home to be with the Lord. He taught me a great deal as I watched and listened to him preach and teach the Gospel for many years. Then my brother in love, Bishop Andy C. Lewter, a great preacher, teacher, and man of God. Then there is T. D. Jakes, who

I've listened to and watched for many years. I have learned much from him, especially how to put a sermon together and deliver it with passion and authority. Next is Benny Hinn, who help me understand the importance of the Holy Spirit and how to go deeper into the spiritual realm.

In 2018, I was summoned by God to write a book on encouragement and prayer. So, I was obedient and wrote my first book. *G's Daily Prayers and Encouragements*, published in 2019, offers uplifting daily devotionals that give readers a daily "dose of medicine." Including scripture, a philosophical quote, and a short prayer to heaven, this dose is designed to help readers prepare themselves daily for any challenge they may face. It's also intended to motivate and make readers stronger and more capable to face each day.

Before I finished writing *G's Daily Prayers and Encouragements*, God tapped me on the shoulder and said, "I'm not done with you yet. I want you to write another book, your life story, and call it *In Deep but Never Too Deep for God*." As I was completing this book, He told me to add *Amazing Grace*.

A lot has happened since my birth in 1951, when we were coming out of oppression as a people to witness all of God's amazing grace in our lives today. Not only did we have our first black president, we also have our first black woman vice president.

First black woman vice president

Kamala Harris, born October 20, 1964, in Oakland California, became the forty-ninth vice president of the United States (2021) in the Democratic administration of President Joe Biden. She was the first woman and the first African American to hold the post. She had previously served in the US Senate (2017–2021) and as attorney general of California (2011–2017).

COVID-19

I was talking on the phone one evening in early March 2019 with one of my good friends for over thirty years by the name of Gary. We fellowshipped together at church and supported each other with dealing with life-on-life's terms. He was complaining of not feeling well and was thinking about going to the hospital. We were just hearing about the COVID-19 virus but never considered the possibility of it having inflicted him. He eventually got so weak he had to be hospitalized. I didn't know I would never talk to or see him again. He was treated and eventually put on a respiratory ventilator. We thought he was going to recover, but he didn't. I was saddened by the news that he'd passed from the virus after about three months in the hospital. Several of my friends and even some relatives lost their lives as well.

The COVID-19 pandemic in the United States was part of a worldwide pandemic of coronavirus disease that broke out in 2019. More than 30 million confirmed cases were reported between 2019 and 2020, resulting in more than 546,000 deaths, the most of any country and the tenth-highest per capita worldwide. The United States had nearly a quarter of the world's cases and a fifth of all deaths. More Americans died from COVID-19 than died during World War II. COVID-19 became the third-leading cause of death in the United States in 2020, behind heart disease and cancer. US life expectancy dropped from 78.8 years in 2019 to 77.8 years in the first half of 2020.

Update as of May 19, 2021 on the progress of vaccinations

Centers for Disease Control and Prevention data show that 60 percent of US adults have received at least one dose of a Covid vaccine. The milestone comes roughly six weeks ahead of July 4, the deadline for President Joe Biden's latest vaccination goal of getting 70 percent of adults to receive one dose or more.

US case counts fell further Tuesday, with the seven-day average of daily new cases now at about 31,200, according to data compiled by Johns Hopkins University.

Of those age eighteen and older, 60 percent are at least partially vaccinated, and in some places, that figure is even higher. In seven states—Vermont, Hawaii, Massachusetts, New Hampshire, Connecticut, Maine, and New Jersey—more than 70 percent of adults have received at least one dose.

The country is reporting an average of 1.8 million vaccinations per day over the past week, federal data shows. That figure has been on a mostly downward trend from its peak level of 3.4 million daily shots on April 13.

The latest seven-day average of daily new Covid cases in the United States is 31,200, according to Hopkins's data. That is down 18 percent from a week prior. The country was reporting an average of more than 71,000 cases per day about a month ago.

More than 587,000 total deaths have been reported in the United States since the start of the pandemic.

So many things were going on in our world, with the pandemic and the black lives movement and the insurrection soon to follow. Many of our black men and women were being murdered by police officers. I woke up one morning, and there it was on the news. One of our black men had been murdered by police, and his death was caught on camera.

George Floyd

On May 25, 2020, George Floyd, a forty-six-year-old black man, was killed in Minneapolis, Minnesota, while being arrested for allegedly using a counterfeit bill. During the arrest, Derek Chauvin, a white police officer with the Minneapolis Police Department, knelt on Floyd's neck for approximately nine minutes and thirty seconds after he was handcuffed and lying face down. Two police officers, J. Alexander Kueng and Thomas Lane, assisted Chauvin in restraining Floyd, while another officer, Tou Thao, prevented bystanders from interfering with the arrest and intervening as events unfolded. Floyd had complained about being unable to breathe prior to being on the ground, but after being restrained he became more distressed and continued to complain about breathing difficulties and the knee on his neck. He expressed the fear he was about to die and called for his mother.

After several minutes passed, Floyd stopped speaking. For a further two minutes, he lay motionless, and Officer Kueng found no pulse when urged to check. Despite this, Chauvin refused pleas to lift his knee until medics told him to.

The following day, after videos made by witnesses and security cameras became public, all four officers were dismissed. Two autopsies found Floyd's death to be a homicide. Chauvin was charged with second-degree unintentional murder, third-degree murder, and second-degree manslaughter.

There were protests across the globe after George Floyd's death. As the protests continued in the United States for weeks in response to his killing, people around the world began to stand with them. From London to Pretoria to Sydney, people took to the streets to express the need for police reform and racial equality. Many held signs that read "Black Lives Matter," while others kneeled. At some protests, marchers stood in silence for the amount of time Floyd struggled to breathe while police officers retained him.

Months later

State of Minnesota v. Derek Michael Chauvin was an American criminal case against former Minneapolis police officer Derek Chauvin, who was convicted of murdering George Floyd during an arrest on May 25, 2020. Chauvin was charged with second-degree murder, third-degree murder, and second-degree manslaughter, which carry penalties of up to forty years of imprisonment. The trial began on March 8, 2021, at the Hennepin County Government Center in Minneapolis, Minnesota. It was the first of two scheduled criminal trials stemming from Floyd's death. It was also the first criminal trial in Minnesota to be entirely televised and the first in state court to be broadcast live. The trial concluded on April 20, 2021, with the jury finding Chauvin guilty of all charges.

Insurrection on the US Capitol

On January 6, 2021, the United States Capitol was stormed during a riot and violent attack against the United States Congress. As I sat and watched the mob of supporters of the seated president attempted to overturn his defeat in the 2020 United States presidential election by disrupting the joint session of Congress assembled to count electoral votes to formalize Joe Biden's victory, I was totally taken by surprise. The capitol complex was locked down, and lawmakers and staff were evacuated while rioters occupied and vandalized the building for several hours. More than 140 people were injured in the storming, and five died during or shortly after it. The event failed to overturn the presidential election, though it was delayed by several hours. The presidential transition leading up to the inauguration of Joe Biden resumed that evening.

This was terribly disturbing to me. I didn't know what to do or how to react or even what to expect in the hours that followed. I wondered if this was the beginning of a civil war in our country. My PSTD increased, and I prepared myself mentally and emotionally for war. Vietnam was back in the front of my mind, and hyper alertness was at its fullness. My mind ran a thousand miles an hour. I was glued to the television watching news as things were unfolding at the state capitol. Finally, they got things under control, and I felt a little relief.

However, I found myself uneasy for about three weeks after the insurrection. My sleep was totally off, and my stress level wasn't good. I didn't get full relief until after I saw the sitting president and his wife board the helicopter to leave the White House.

Tulsa race massacre

As I bring my autobiography to completion, it is Memorial Day 2021. A century ago this week, the wealthiest US black community was burned to the ground.

Most of us had never heard of this tragedy that had happened over a hundred years ago. Until news reports brought it to light, I was totally unaware of this profound event in our history.

At the turn of the twentieth century, the Greenwood District of Tulsa, Oklahoma, became one of the first communities in the country to thrive with black entrepreneurial businesses. The prosperous town, founded by many descendants of slaves, earned a reputation as the Black Wall Street of America and became a harbor for African Americans in a highly segregated city under Jim Crow laws.

On May 31, 1921, a white mob turned Greenwood upside down in one of the worst racial massacres in US history. In a matter of hours, thirty-five square blocks of the vibrant black community were turned into smoldering ashes. Countless black people were killed— estimates ranged from fifty-five to more than three hundred—and a thousand homes and businesses were looted and set on fire.

Yet for the longest time, the massacre received scant mention in newspapers, textbooks, and civil and governmental conversations. It wasn't until 2000 that the slaughter was included in the Oklahoma public schools' curriculum, and it didn't enter American history textbooks until recent years. The 1921 Tulsa Race Riot Commission was formed to investigate in 1997 and officially released a report in 2000.

"The massacre was actively covered up with the white community in Tulsa for nearly a half century," said Scott Ellsworth, a professor of Afro American and African studies at the University of Michigan and author of *The Groundbreaking* about the Tulsa massacre.

"When I started my research in the 1970s, I discovered that official National Guard reports and other documents were all missing," Ellsworth said. "Tulsa's two daily white newspapers, they went out of their way for decades not to mention the massacre. Researchers who would try to do work on this as late as the early 1970s had their lives threatened and had their career threatened."

In the week following the massacre, Tulsa's chief of police ordered his officers to go to all the photography studios in Tulsa and confiscate all the pictures taken of the carnage, Ellsworth said.

Some photos, which were later discovered and became the materials the Oklahoma Commission used to study the massacre, eventually landed in the lap of Michelle Place at Tulsa Historical Society and Museum in 2001. "It took me about four days to get through the box because the photographs were so horrific. I had never seen those kinds of pictures before," Place said. "I didn't know anything about the riot before I came to work here. I never heard of it. Since I have been here, I've been at my desk to guard them to the very best of my ability."

The Tulsa Museum was founded in the late 1990s, but visitors couldn't find a trace of the race massacre until 2012 when Place became executive director, determined to tell all of Tulsa's stories. A digital collection of the photographs was eventually made available for viewing online.

"There's still a significant number of people in our community who don't want to look at it, who don't want to talk about it," Place said.

Not only did Tulsa city officials cover up the bloodbath, they also deliberately shifted the narrative of the massacre by calling it a "riot" and blaming the black community for what went down, according to Alicia Odewale, an archaeologist at University of Tulsa.

The massacre wasn't discussed publicly in the African American community either for a long time—first, out of fear; if it happened once, it could happen again.

"You are seeing the perpetrators walking freely on the streets," Odewale said. "You are in the Jim Crow South, and there are racial terrors happening across the country at this time. They are protecting themselves for a reason."

Moreover, for survivors, this was a profoundly traumatic event. And much like Holocaust survivors and World War II veterans, many did not want to burden their children and grandchildren with the horrible memories.

Ellsworth said he knows of descendants of massacre survivors who didn't find out about it until they were in their forties and fifties.

"The silence is layered just as the trauma is layered," Odewale said. "The historical trauma is real, and that trauma lingers especially because there's no justice, no accountability and no reparation or monetary compensation."

On May 31, 1921, Dick Rowland, a nineteen-year-old black shoe shiner, tripped and fell in an elevator. His hand accidentally caught the shoulder of Sarah Page, a white seventeen-year-old operator. Page screamed, and Rowland was seen running away.

Police were summoned, but Page refused to press charges. However, by that afternoon, there were already talks of lynching Rowland on the streets of white Tulsa. The tension then escalated after the white newspaper *Tulsa Tribune* ran a front-page story entitled "Nab for Attacking Girl in Elevator," which accused Rowland of stalking, assault, and rape.

In the *Tribune*, there was also a now-lost editorial entitled "To Lynch Tonight," according to Ellsworth. When the Works Progress Administration went to microfilm the old issues of the Tribune in the 1930s, the op-ed had already been torn out of the newspaper,

Ellsworth said. Many believe the newspaper coverage played a part in sparking the massacre.

For Black Tulsans, the massacre resulted in a decline in home ownership, occupational status, and educational attainment that lasted through the 1940s, according to a recent study led by Harvard University's Alex Albright. Today, there are only a few black businesses on the single remaining block in the Greenwood district once hailed as the Black Wall Street.

This month, three survivors of the 1921 massacre—ages 100, 106, and 107—appeared before a congressional committee, and a Georgia congressman introduced a bill that would make it easier for them to seek reparations.

Meanwhile, historians and archaeologists continued to unearth what was lost for decades. In October, a mass grave in an Oklahoma cemetery was discovered that could be the remains of at least a dozen identified and unidentified African American massacre victims.

"We are able to look for signs of survival and signs of lives. And really look for those remnants of built Greenwood and not just about how they died," Odewale said. "Greenwood never left."

A century after a white mob destroyed a vibrant African American community in Tulsa, Oklahoma, torching hundreds of homes and indiscriminately shooting people in the streets, President Biden told a crowd of survivors and their families that the story of the massacre "would be known in full view."

It was the first time a president had visited the area to address what had happened a hundred years ago in Greenwood—the site of one of the worst outbreaks of racist violence in American history but one that went largely ignored in history books.

"For much too long, the history of what took place here was told in silence," Mr. Biden told the crowd. "While darkness can hide much, it erases nothing."

Mr. Biden, who has made racial equity and justice central themes of his presidency, was there to shed light on a painful part of the country's history, by recalling in detail the horror that occurred between May 31 and June 1 in 1921, when angry whites descended on Greenwood, a prosperous part of Tulsa known as Black Wall Street, killing as many as three hundred people and destroying more than 1,250 homes.

"My fellow Americans, this was not a riot," Mr. Biden said, as people in the crowd rose to their feet. "This was a massacre."

A man was strapped to a pickup truck and dragged through the street, the president said. The bodies of a murdered family were draped over the fence outside their home. An older couple was shot while praying.

"We do ourselves no favors by pretending none of this ever happened," Mr. Biden told the crowd in Tulsa. "We should know the good, the bad, everything. That is what great nations do. They come to terms with their dark sides."

Mr. Biden's visit was also intended to highlight steps his administration is taking to close the wealth gap between black and white people in the United States, even as activists criticized him for not going far enough to correct historical wrongs and put the disadvantaged on equal footing.

He announced several initiatives to reduce racial disparities, including a pledge to boost federal contracts to minority-owned businesses by 50 percent and a rollback of two Trump-era actions that have hamstrung fair housing laws.

Before he delivered remarks, Mr. Biden met privately with survivors of the massacre, each between the ages of 101 and 107, whom he mentioned throughout his speech.

Epilogue

I pray that this book will be a blessing to you and give you courage and hope that, no matter what live throws your way, it is never too hard for God to handle.

In deep but never too deep for God' amazing grace

In my life, I found myself in deep waters several times, but God came to my rescue and made a way for me. The times when I just wanted to give up and throw in the towel, I could hear a soft whisper in my spirit: "Hold on, my son. Hold on to your faith. Remember my Words of encouragement that say, I will never leave nor forsake you." Most of my life has been a struggle. But even during those times, I was able to find some happiness and eventually joy in my latter days.

My wife, my son and daughter, and my grandchildren brought me the most joy I could ever receive outside the great connection I have with my Lord and Savior Jesus the Christ. My life experiences are a gift from God. I wouldn't change anything I had to go through. There have been some weary days and sleepless nights, some pain and sorrow and grief. I've made plenty of mistakes, some I'll never get the opportunity to make direct amends for, but God has made a way for me to make those amends indirectly.

When all is said and done on this side of heaven for me (I am in no hurry), please don't say I gave up. Just say I gave in to God's will. Don't say I lost the battle, for the battle was the Lord's. Please don't say how good I was; simply say I did my best to do what was right.

Please don't give me wings or halos; that is for God to do. I want no more than I deserve, no extras, just my due. Please don't give me flowers or talk in harsh tones. Don't be concerned about what might have been. When you draw a picture of me, my son Monzique, don't draw me as a saint. I've done some good and bad, so use all your paint—not just the bright and light tones; use some gray and dark. In fact, don't put me down on canvas; paint me in your heart.

My daughter Ariel, don't just remember the struggles of life but remember the good times as well. For life is full of many things, some happy and some sad. Think about the times when we would run together and hold hands, laugh, and enjoy life together.

My sister, Pat; brother Walter; wife, Tonya, and all relatives, friends, and readers of this book, if I can impress one thing upon you, please remember life is very short, even in its longest, so love one another and remember: *God is in charge.*